CHILDREN IN JAIL

CHILDREN IN JAIL

Seven
Lessons
in
American
Justice

THOMAS J. COTTLE

Beacon Press *Boston*

To the memory of
BABETTE SCHILLER SPIEGEL

Copyright © 1977 by Thomas J. Cottle

Beacon Press books are published under the auspices of the Unitarian Universalist Association

Published simultaneously in Canada by Fitzhenry & Whiteside Limited, Toronto

All rights reserved

Printed in the United States of America

(hardcover) 9 8 7 6 5 4 3 2

Library of Congress Cataloging in Publication Data

Cottle, Thomas J
    Children in jail.
    1. Juvenile delinquency—United States—Case studies.
2. Juvenlie corrections—United States—Case studies.
I. Title.
HV9104.C59   365'.42'0973   75-77440
ISBN 0-8070-0492-8

Contents

v

Acknowledgments

I wish to thank, first, the young people whose words appear in this book, and their parents, or in some cases guardians, all of whom granted permission for their words to be made public. Let me thank, too, the penal institutions, their directors, and staff, who allowed me to undertake the work in the first place and encouraged me as it progressed.

For their special form of support, I thank The Children's Defense Fund of the Washington Research Project where, in many respects, the work began; the Guggenheim Foundation of New York, Nicholas Rey, President; and The Tavistock Center and Hampstead Child Therapy Clinic, London.

In addition, many people should be singled out for their significant contribution to the book. They include, Paul Barker, Rochelle Beck, Ray Bentley, my treasured editor; Oliver W. Holmes, Michael I. Kessler, Jennifer King, Sharon Liburd, Sally Makacynas, Gerald M. Platt, Viviette Reynell, Fred Stern, John Stokes, Paul M. Strudler, and always my partner, Kay M. Cottle.

The final acknowledgment is an expression of gratitude and appreciation to three women who have worked, it seems, all their lives, in behalf of children. They are Miss Anna Freud, Marian Wright Edelman, and Babette Schiller Spiegel, to whom the book is dedicated.

Introduction: They Haven't Always Been in Jail

According to statistics prepared by the Law Enforcement Assistance Administration, there are approximately 160,000 people in jail throughout the United States on any given day. If one considers turnover rates, as many as five and a half million men and women are in jail in the course of one year. Of those arrested for crimes of violence, about 22 percent are children under the age of eighteen. Of those arrested for property offenses, 50 percent are children under eighteen. While these last figures may seem high to some people, it is often said that children represent about 50 percent of all people arrested. Clearly they do not. Indeed, the figures for crimes committed by children and the number of children in jail in the United States are far from clear.

Studies recently completed by the Children's Defense Fund of the Washington Research Project reveal that more than 900,000 American children are jailed in the course of a year. New York State alone had almost 6,000 juveniles in jail in 1970. As shocking as these figures are, they clearly amount to an underestimation, since there is no way of knowing with precision the number of children in detention centers or held in jail awaiting trial. These children too are technically in jail, although they often are not so considered in official surveys. Indeed, the Children's Defense Fund, through interviews, learned that many jails which detained juveniles did not report these children when the National Jail Census of 1970 was conducted. Furthermore, some prison officials did not consider a child held for several days in a police lockup to be an official case of incarceration.

The Children's Defense Fund study indicates that, of the children in jail, the majority were white boys, although there were also a disproportionate number of minority children. The average age of the jailed child was between sixteen and seventeen, although it is not uncommon to find children as young as twelve or thirteen. It is also not uncommon to find children assigned to jails where adults are imprisoned despite laws preventing this action. Indeed it has long been argued that people under the age of eighteen should not be sentenced to jail and that worthwhile alternative rehabilitative, educational, and vocational programs be established. Yet, in the decade from 1950 to 1960, the number of children in jail increased by almost 90 percent. The average length of time a child is held in jail is about six days, yet the Children's Defense Fund found that the period of incarceration was not directly related to the period stipulated by state law. It is obvious, therefore, that children's rights are regularly being abrogated in the process of their being arrested, charged, arraigned, and sentenced to jail.

Contrary to popular belief, the large majority of children in jail studied by the Children's Defense Fund had not been charged with committing a violent crime. Less than 20 percent in fact were jailed for some violent act. Mainly, they had committed so-called property offenses and what the law considers minor behavioral violations. More than 15 percent of the children were in jail for so-called status offenses, which are not considered criminal if committed by an adult. These include truancy, running away, and the infamous charge of being incorrigible. It must also be pointed out that a great many children—although it is impossible to determine exactly how many—are in jail for protective custody. That is, no official charge has been made. Some children are jailed because they have been diagnosed as being mentally retarded or ill. While most of these children are released from jail after a brief period of time, there are many cases of children kept in protective custody for as long as five years.

No one needs to be told that jails serve no positive function for the individual, particularly when that individual is a child. The reason for incarceration is to remove the person from society. But prison recidivism rates make it evident that incarceration by itself rarely deters criminal action. The notion that prison is therapy is preposterous. Jail means punishment and abuse, rarely protection or treatment. The expression that prison teaches crime and *makes* criminals as often as it *takes* them is especially appropriate in the case of young people. But this is not surprising, for anyone who has ever visited city or county jails, where the majority of children are incarcerated, can see, and smell, in a moment why a jail can only do harm to a child.

To begin with, most jails are old and offer the worst physical facilities imaginable. Jails are understaffed, and very few staff members have had any special experience or training in treating young people. Furthermore, many jails do not offer any sort of program that could possibly be seen as rehabilitative. Consider in this regard the following statistics reported in the 1970 National Jail Census.

Combined, there are 1,021 city and county jails in cities or towns of over 25,000 people in the states of Florida, Georgia, Indiana, Maryland, New Jersey, Ohio, South Carolina, Texas, and Virginia. Of these, one can find recreational facilities in less than 13 percent, educational facilities in less than 10 percent, medical facilities in almost exactly 50 percent. While percentages can be misleading, there is nothing misleading about the facts that only 2.7 percent of Ohio's 112 city and county jails have educational facilities or that 38.6 percent of South Carolina's 101 jails have no medical facilities (some of these are merely first-aid kits) or that 2.6 percent of Texas's 265 jails have recreational facilities. Thirty percent of Texas city and county jails have no prisoner visiting facilities!

In the same census, jail administrators were asked to describe their "locally sponsored rehabilitative services and programs." While it would be very difficult to confirm the reports of the respective jails, the figures themselves were hardly encouraging. About 11 percent of jails studied reported group counseling and remedial education programs. Vocational training was reported in 14 percent; job development and placement in 12.5 percent; alcoholic treatment in 35 percent; drug addiction treatment programs in 27 percent. Yet 60 percent of the jails offered religious services. One wonders whether these statistics would change significantly if the responsibility for jail control and maintenance lay with the federal government rather than with town, city, and county governments.

While many people are well aware of these statistics and the conditions of jails, some cannot find in themselves sympathy for imprisoned men and women. While their feelings may soften on the issue of children in jail, they might argue that people who commit crimes must be tried and, if found guilty, sentenced, even if they are children. Even the most radical proponent of prison reform would insist that acts committed by children against persons and property cannot be condoned. Something must be done, but the facts speak for themselves. Incarceration rarely prevents further crime. In the short and long run, jails solve little. They do perform one significant function: by isolating so-called criminals, the rest of us are no longer in danger of "attack" by these people. Moreover, we need not think of them as people; we do not think of them. They exist solely in terms of our labels and designations. They are prisoners, inmates, delinquents, criminals—no longer men and women, no longer boys and girls. And just as their human qualities are assaulted in prison, so too is their humanness taken away by us as we label and sequester them. They have no faces, no names, they are known by numbers, and by the very statistics we have just examined. Their present and future identity is defined in the context of jail, their past identity is automatically recorded in terms of their criminal action. It is not absurd to say that some people imagine delinquent youths as people who spend every waking hour of their lives either contemplating or performing some criminal activity, and every sleeping hour dreaming of crime. Sadly, there is little popular information about these children in jail, and so the stereotypes and prejudicial attitudes remain. Certainly they remained with me when I began to do the research for this book.

For many years in my work with families in various American cities, I had spoken with young people who had been in jail or had friends in jail. But it was not until much later that I made arrangements to speak with children while they were serving jail sentences or waiting in jail for their trials to begin. Originally, the purpose of my work was to gather information from the children about conditions of jails and generally about life in jail. As someone who has always believed that no one can speak more eloquently about another person's life than the person himself or herself, I was eager to begin my interviews with the children in jail who, along with their families, had granted permission for the interviews. To my surprise, the initial work went so slowly, so poorly in fact, I resolved to give up the project entirely. The young men and women were willing to meet with me, but there was nothing they had to say. Indeed, we would often sit silently in the visiting room of their jail looking at one another as if we spoke different languages. In those moments, my own prejudicial beliefs about so-called delinquent youths could not have been more prominent in my thinking.

Finally, on the verge of telling one boy that I would no longer be visiting him, since apparently he either had nothing to say or preferred not to speak with *me*, the boy made a simple suggestion. "Why not ask me to talk about other things in my life instead of just my life in here," he said. "I haven't *always* been in jail, you know." It was perfectly true. I had been treating these young people as if they were nothing more than criminals, or informants about life in jail. But the boy's message was even more complicated than I first had heard, for besides reminding me that a person is far more than a prisoner, the experience of being in jail can be so terrifying and brutal that one is unable to speak about it for a long time, if ever.

Gradually, the topics of our conversations shifted to their childhood, their families, school, friends, a whole range of issues, and, not surprisingly, the energy and eloquence that always comes forth when people speak about themselves returned in the words of the children in jail. There was nothing in the physical environment that encouraged them.

The visiting rooms were at best sterile, sanitized chambers, where privacy was denied and where everything from the architecture to the lights and sounds, and of course my own presence, enhanced the young people's feelings of shame.

The following profiles of children in jail are the result of several years of conversations, most of them held in jails. All names are fictitious, and for the protection of the children, their families, and fellow prisoners, names of cities, states, and penal institutions are not listed in the text. I guarantee those who speak with me anonymity in all my work. Even when they ask to have their names publicized, I insist on preserving confidentiality. In this one instance, while anonymity has an obvious necessity, I feel uncomfortable, for once again the identity of these young people has been masked. Still, I hope that even with fictitious names, their words will sound as real and alive to the reader as they did when I first heard them, and again when I had the privilege of recording them for this book.

1

That Kid Will End Up Killing Somebody

Bobbie Dijon was always the tallest girl in her class; only a few boys were taller. Some of the children laughed at her in third and fourth and fifth grade. But by the time she was twelve, she was so strong and so big, nobody ever teased her for they feared that Bobbie would haul off and pound them with her fists, which she was known to do. It was not, her teachers said, that she was a tough girl, or a bad girl. There was a tough part of her, but it was a small part that lived inside her, content not to show itself unless seriously provoked. But when provoked, it came out, and Bobbie Dijon was transformed into a fighting animal, seemingly fearless, perhaps irrational as well.

It is often said that children who get into trouble with the law, perhaps even end up in jail, are tough kids who have never experienced a tender friendship and therefore do not know the meaning of tenderness. They just seem to be tough all the time. They act tough, talk tough, eat tough, maybe even sleep tough. It's an intriguing description of children but it surely does not seem relevant in the case of Bobbie Dijon. One felt in looking at her that she was not the type to duck away from a fight, but she hardly gave the appearance of someone openly looking for trouble or physical violence. As she grew older and saw how much taller she was than most of her friends, she began to slouch. By thrusting her head forward and bending over slightly at the waist, she probably reduced her height by five inches. She recognized the appearance of grace that had been lost by hunching up in this manner, but it was better, she said, than standing taller than everybody and becoming so conspicuous. She said too she hated the feeling of being a giraffe. She would have preferred to resemble a tiger.

She minds being seen by some people as a sort of freak, although the students in the schools she has attended have learned not to tease her about it. It bothers her too that she is the only one in her family who could be considered tall. The other three children are of normal height, possibly even a bit shorter than normal. For a long while Bobbie could not understand how this could be. When she was nine the mystery of her height was settled. It was then she learned that her real father was not the man her mother was living with, the man she called Daddy. It turned out that Bobbie's older sister Beverly, who was the first born, and her brother Timmy were the children of one father, while her younger sister Diane was the daughter of another father, the one Bobbie called Daddy. Marianne Dijon had had four children with three men. When Bobbie was nine years old, she learned the truth of her real father and discovered that her brother was really a half brother and her sisters half sisters.

"It was funny the way I sort of heard what my mother was saying. Like, I knew what she was telling me. She was saying, this guy Gerald isn't your father. I could take that. I knew lots of kids living with people who weren't their real mothers and fathers. I was a little surprised. You had to be a little surprised to get news like that. How do you do. This isn't your father. I guess the second shock got me more, which was that my mother hadn't even talked to my real father since, well, from when I was born. And he hadn't even come to see me. She got pregnant and he stayed around. I suppose Beverly probably thought that he was *her* father. Fact is, when my mother told me about my real father I don't even know whether Bev and Timmy knew anything about their real father. Maybe they did and forgot, or maybe somebody told them not to tell nobody. I think my mother made a mistake not telling us. I'd have still called him Daddy, only I would have known. I mean I would have liked to know. A child should know.

"But anyway, I took the news all right, I suppose. Then the next day I did sort of a dumb thing. Like, my mother told me in the night, before I went to bed. Maybe I was upset but I can't remember. You'd think you'd never forget news like that 'cause it's only going to happen to you once in your life, but I forgot. So I went to bed and went to school the next day like everything was fine and like, first thing in the morning there's this girl Petie something, nice kid, I liked her only I thought she said something about my being tall. I heard her giggling with her friends about how I was some sort of giraffe. So I walked up to her and hit her a shot right in the face. I cut her eye and broke off a tooth of hers. I wasn't even that mad. You know how sometimes you get burning up with being mad. I wasn't that way at all. It was like boom, it came and went. You couldn't even see it. I just walked up to her and hit her. It was like the teacher saying, 'Bobbie, would you please go down the hall and turn the light switch on.' So you take a few steps, hit the switch, walk back. You know how people say, like, something snapped inside? I guess something snapped inside. But I never heard it or saw it.

"But there *was* something I did know about when I hit her. The second my fist hit her I knew I was angry about what my mother had told us the night before. I knew it. Lots of kids razzed me about being a girl basketball player and I didn't hit 'em or nothing. If I did I'd have been hitting everybody I ever passed on the street. That one time I knew it was because I didn't know my father and probably never was going to know him. It made me mad, maybe 'cause I knew I couldn't do nothing about it. Of course I must have made the connection somewhere about why I *was* so tall. It must have been 'cause my father, whoever the hell he was— are you listening to me Father out there somewhere?—must have been a real tall guy. I asked my mother, lots of times, was he tall? 'I don't know,' she goes. 'I can't remember, I think so.' That makes a kid feel good, don't it. Have so many Ma, did you? But hell, she had it just as tough. I don't think she knew her real father or mother. Nobody ever told her straight about anything in her life. She'd had three abortions by the time she was fifteen. Three! And you can imagine how they must have done 'em in those days! With a fork and a carpenter's saw if the woman was lucky. My mom was a whore when she was fourteen. Had to. Had no other way to go. Parents don't support you, nobody's going to feed you, nobody's about to give a poor slob of a girl with no education a job where she can make enough money to support herself. She didn't have a skill in the world, 'cept lying on a bed somewhere and let men crawl over her like ants on the old proverbial anthill!

" 'Tell me Mrs. Dijon, why did you become a prostitute?' 'Well, you see, sir, after I finished college, I decided I would take a bit of a vacation. I had been traveling in Europe trying to decide what I should do with the rest of my life. Should I become a doctor or a lawyer or perhaps just settle for a job in the government. Well, I simply couldn't make up my mind with all these wonderful things I could do so I said to myself, how about becoming a prostitute. I could make a lot of money and think of all the interesting people I would meet, and all you have to do is lie around all day and let the world come to you. And if you make a few mistakes and a few kids slip through by accident, you can always keep them in a back room where nobody sees them and keep your business going just like before. You just pull down the blinds and keep your nice little room dark so all the people coming to see you don't have to get sick to their stomach seeing how scarred up you've gotten by the time you're twenty-one!' "

In time the little bit of anger Bobbie Dijon kept inside her seemed to grow. She hid it from people as best she could, but by the time she was thirteen she was known as the girl with the atomic temper. She could go for weeks acting as if she were the nicest girl in the world, but then suddenly, somebody would touch that spot of anger and she would erupt. Often her explosions ended up with her getting hurt more seriously than the intended victim. When she was twelve, Bobbie went after a boy three years older. Nobody ever learned what he had said or done. It was in one of the school corridors early in the morning, before classes started. Bobbie was walking with a bunch of girls and must have heard something. Suddenly she ran down the hall and lunged at one of the boys near the drinking fountain. She caught him full force with her fist on the side of his head, but somehow he was barely stunned. Then, in one movement, he spun her around and cracked her with both hands together on the jaw and the left side of her neck. His blow knocked her out and she fell in a heap as though she had been killed.

Bucky Harrold's retaliation had broken Bobbie's jaw. For three weeks she lay in a hospital bed not knowing whether she would ever again speak properly. Her mother never visited her. Marianne Dijon said if her daughter "was hurt in an accident she would visit her every free hour of the day and night. But if Bobbie had been hurt because for no reason she decided to pick a fight with a kid three years older than her and probably ten times as strong she'd have to suffer all by her lonesome."

Bobbie had no visitors in the hospital for the first four days, her mother not even telling Beverly or Timmy where she was. Her first visitor was Bucky Harrold.

"Poor Bucky. He came in looking like he'd lost the fight 'stead of me. Said he'd never hit no girl before. He really looked like a sick old dog or something. I almost laughed when I saw him looking so sad and apologizing to me. But I wanted to cry too 'cause like the only friend I had in the world, on that one day, was the guy I'd tried to hurt. He told me the only reason he came to see me was 'cause his mother made him. He didn't have to say that but I forgave him. Bucky Harrold and I are a lot alike, I suppose. He'll fight someone at the drop of a hat the way I do. He can be plenty mean. But the rest of the time he's so quiet and sad looking, you'd think he'd fall over if anybody blew hard enough in his direction. I guess maybe I'm the same way. I think I see me like everybody does. I'm sad most of the time and angry the rest of the time.

"A social worker who came to see my mother once, Mrs. Biondi, she told my mother that after studying all of us, or whatever she called it, interviewing us, that I was the nicest because I talked the most to her, but if she had to bet on me, she'd bet I'd end up killing somebody 'cause I seemed so angry. My mother told her she was crazy. Timmy, she said, was the guy who was going to be a murderer if, God forbid, there had to be a murderer. But *I* thought Mrs. Biondi was right, even though I didn't think it was nice of her to say that since she didn't even know us. I mean, you don't go into someone's home for a couple of hours and tell their mother, 'I think Bobbie's going to end up being a murderer someday, Mrs. Dijon, even though she's kind of not a bad kid now.' Maybe that's the way those people are taught to do their work, but if you ask me, I think what she said could be taken like kind of a challenge. I don't need no professional social worker to tell me I'd like to kill somebody. I've wanted to kill my old man since I found out I didn't even know who he was. I know damn well if somebody introduced me to the man right now I'd go after him. I would too. I'd probably get my face busted like old Bucky Harrold done to me, but I'd take him on. I would too.

"They got lots of guys teaching that the worst criminals in the world are the guys who murder or rape people. No one's saying they aren't bad people. But deep down they're sick people. People only do horrible things like that when they're sick. For me, the worst guys are the guys like my father because of one important thing: they make their old lady pregnant, then the woman has her baby and they leave. The kid grows up never even knowing who their father is, or thinking, like in my case, that the guy they call Daddy is their father. These guys kill people almost like murderers. They ruin people's lives if the people aren't strong. But they never get caught. You got a guy in prison for murdering somebody, he's been caught, he's paying the price for what he did. But my father's never been caught. And he better not let me catch him."

No one is able to escape the reputation others impose upon them. All reputations probably have some truth to them, but they are also comprised of dreams and wishes, envies, and often outright adoration and revulsion. Bobbie Dijon never escaped the reputation she carried when she was ten years old. She was a fighter, a cauldron of anger. No matter who it was, they saw the shadowy outlines of the fire buried in her soul. Her teachers in the three schools she attended claimed the reputation was perfectly accurate. "Any minute she could just go," one of them said, referring to the mercurial way, the incendiary spirit. If the teachers did not recognize the fire at first glance, or even discover it after several months of having Bobbie Dijon in their classes, then they learned about it soon enough from reading her school records. Everywhere she went she was seen as the fire bomb, the potential killer, the girl who should have been a boy, the child destined to suffer all her life but who resolved long ago that if she were going down, she would take as many people with her as she could.

The reputation did not escape the social work agency that worked in the Dijons's neighborhood, one of the poorest areas of the city, an area known for its high rate of juvenile crime. Several social workers visited with the Dijon family—once when Marianne took it into her head to adopt a child, an idea that was promptly extinguished; another time when the police received a report that Marianne had beaten Diane. The child had been rushed to the hospital where she was treated for abrasions. She had been beaten by someone, but it was not Marianne, for she had spent the day with friends miles away.

In fact, the beating of Diane remained a mystery. Bobbie insisted it was a neighbor, a man named Colsey who lived upstairs. Ben Colsey used to get drunk in the middle of the morning so that by noon he would be heard screaming and ranting. Since he lived alone there was never anyone at home to quiet or constrain him. Sometimes the drinking brought out his rage, and he would come barging down the stairs, banging on his neighbors' doors; they all knew better than to let him in. Bobbie, and many others, assumed that he found the Dijon door unlocked, and when he entered he saw Diane, who was then two years old. Maybe he hit her, maybe he just fell over on her. The police never proved anything. Indeed they seemed to be spending most of their time trying to convince the social workers that it was Marianne who had hit her daughter.

With the beating of Diane and the run-of-the-mill trouble that the other Dijon children fell into, there seemed to be a social worker coming to the Dijon household every other day. Bobbie took a great liking to one, a woman named Patsy Monahan. Patsy had been well versed in the subject of Bobbie's hot temper. She had spoken to several of Bobbie's teachers and to police at the precinct station several blocks away. "Bobbie Dijon," the police would say, "the human fireball. Kid's going to end up behind bars one of these days. Every time you see a kid like that you want to pick them up and put them behind bars, for *their* sake." Patsy Monahan always asked whether Bobbie had been involved in criminal activities. The police answered, "No, but she will be. She will be." You could predict it by two things, they said. Talk to her and you could see it in her eyes. She had the look of a killer. You saw it in the coldness of her eyes, the stare that went right through you as if you weren't even standing in front of her. And if you never met her, then all you had to know was who she was running around with. Take a look at any of those kids and you could see all of them leading each other right down the road to the old reformatory. That kid Dijon, they all said, should be behind bars. It would save everybody a lot of trouble, and it might even save the life of some innocent person somewhere. That was when Bobbie was thirteen.

Ironically, the closer Bobbie got to Patsy Monahan and felt freer about expressing all that made her at the same time sad and furious, the closer she edged to criminal acts. She began shoplifting, first on an occasional basis but later as a regular habit until she "hit the stores" as often as four days a week. Then there were some fights, sometimes with individual girls, but later with entire groups of young people. There was no doubt that she had fallen in with a group of young people who, while they never called themselves an organized club, acted much in the manner of what the police called gangs.

Bobbie spoke openly with Patsy about robberies her friends had committed, always denying that she had participated in anything. She would sit in the chair in front of the living room windows or take walks with Patsy, slumping over slightly so as not to seem so tall, pushing her hair away from her eyes, a gesture that had become almost a tic. Her friends kidded her about it. She's got her hand in her hair even when she sleeps, they would chide her. She's even afraid to go swimming in the summer because she can't stand her hair falling over her face and she refuses to wear a bathing cap. But they also said that when Bobbie Dijon was in a fight, she didn't worry about her hair, unless of course her opponent made the mistake of pulling it. That seemed to make her explode. "If you have to get in a fight with Bobbie Dijon," one of her friends said, "go clean. Go for the face, for the belly, but don't pull the hair, it takes her apart. She'll come at you like a hundred screaming lions and claw you. She'd bite you to death with her teeth if she had to. She'll die doing it, but she'll win. *You'll* die a long time before *she* does."

Bobbie Dijon was getting to be quite the celebrity in her neighborhood. The Tall Tiger, the police called her. That was followed by the standard remark, "It's just a matter of time before . . ." But nobody ever said before what. Then, late one Sunday night, with snow on the ground and the weather so cold one could barely walk ten steps without having to go indoors, Bobbie Dijon and a friend named Rosalind Warkovsky, who was supposed to be a distant cousin of Bucky Harrold's, were picked up by the police. The girls, both of them six months short of their fifteenth birthdays, were wanted for questioning. They were pushed into the back of a police car where a policeman who Bobbie later said looked young enough to be her own age, read them their rights. The girls were furious, but they giggled when Officer Kierren read to them from a pad of paper. It made them think they had been thrown into the middle of a television show. When they became serious again, Bobbie told the officers they had no right arresting her and Rosalind unless the police could tell them exactly what crime they were supposed to have committed. In the car, the police said nothing.

At the police station, the story became clear. At approximately ten thirty that evening, a man was found dead in the front hall of the apartment building in which the Dijons and five other families lived. None of the Dijons could be located, a fact that puzzled the police, especially because on a Sunday night, most families with school-age children get ready for bed early. Another puzzling fact was that the dead man was Ben Colsey who many neighbors had said repeatedly argued with the Dijon girl, the tall one who spent her time fighting with people, including pathetic old drunks like Ben Colsey, and pushing her hair out of her eyes. The police had learned that on at least three occasions Bobbie Dijon had engaged in long arguments with Ben Colsey, whom she called a filthy old man.

"Ben Colsey did two things in his life when he wasn't sleeping," Bobbie said. "He drank and he tried to screw anything he could find that would hold still long enough. Man tried to rape me when I was twelve. Couldn't believe I was that young, he kept saying, 'cause I was so tall. Liar! He knew exactly how old I was. Six months later he tried again. I almost broke his skull in with a tray my mother used to put her plants on. I grabbed it and bashed him on the head with it. He never reported what happened, even to the people at the hospital, 'cause he knew what they'd find out about him. Filthy old man. My mother got so angry she told him she'd do it free for him if he'd stay away from her daughters. She knew if he'd come after me like he did, he'd go after Diane by the time she was eleven. Diane looks a lot older than she is, too. But Ben Colsey became so proper all of a sudden. He told my mother he never pays for his women, doesn't have to. Sure he doesn't have to. He just rapes the ones who say no. Brave man, has to get drunk and pick on girls in the sixth grade!"

It was true that Ben Colsey was known as a complete washout, a reprobate of the first order. The police had been watching him for months. But he did not kill himself. He had been bludgeoned and chained to death in a park, then dragged into the entrance hall of the Dijon apartment building, several blocks away. The tracks in the snow made all this clear. The police reasoned that the assailants knew where he lived and presumably wanted to get him to his apartment, but something scared them off.

"Perhaps they couldn't carry him no more," Rosalind Warkovsky suggested. She was tittering with laughter, for she had never even heard of Ben Colsey and knew she would be released.

"Maybe it was a bunch of girls who did it," the police retorted. "Maybe they didn't have the strength to carry the dead man up the stairs. Ever think of that!"

"If they were strong enough to drag him like you said,"

Rosalind argued, "they could have put him on the roof. You guys better make up your minds, get your stories together."

"And you better clean up your own act, girlie," one of the policemen shot back.

Bobbie Dijon said nothing. She slumped in the chair in the police station a half mile from her home thinking about whom she would telephone if the police ever got around to allowing her that infamous single phone call. She could always tell them she wished to speak to her father and nobody else. And since nobody knew where her father was, whether he was even alive, the police would have to let her go. But she was angry with her mother for not being there. Beverly was out of the city and God only knew where Timmy and Diane were. But why did her mother have to be out so much. She must be at the Croyden, Bobbie thought, going into the hotel rooms of the businessmen so the poor little angels wouldn't get their feet wet and catch cold chasing whores all over the city. Maybe she should give them an aspirin or an Alka Seltzer when they're done.

On Monday morning, Bobbie Dijon and Rosalind Warkovsky were arraigned in a city court. They were being held as accomplices to the murder of Benjamin Arnold Colsey of 1253 South Leighton Avenue. As the judge spoke and the bailiff moved silently about the huge courtroom, Bobbie Dijon could think of only one thing! How was it she never knew that Colsey's middle name was Arnold. What a strange love, the neighborhood kids used to call him. They laughed their heads off watching him stagger in and out the front door, and they bet he couldn't make it up the stairs without falling ten times. Cozy Colsey, the man who took from the dole and anyone else he could cheat.

The high point of Ben Colsey's life was a period of three women to pimp for. He referred to them as his stable and they paid him 25 percent of every trick. Still on the dole, he took his stable money and strutted about Wexler and Pines Streets as if he were a king. Then the women began to cheat on him. He threatened them and they laughed in his face. One by one they told him they were only doing him a favor, that they could drop him in a minute. He told them he'd like to see them try. So they quit giving him his take and one morning, when it was still dark, he broke into one of their apartments and assaulted a young woman named Darlene with a broken bottle. Fortunately for her, Ben Colsey was so drunk he could barely stand. He was no match for Darlene, although she received a cut on her belly during the fight, before she knocked him out by swatting him several times on the head with a man's shoe. Bobbie Dijon knew this story well, Darlene being the street name for her own sister Beverly. Until that night, a year and a half before her arraignment, Marianne Dijon had had no knowledge that her eldest daughter was following in her footsteps.

Bobbie Dijon was placed in prison to await her trial. The police grew increasingly uncertain about Rosalind Warkovsky's role in the murder of Ben Colsey. Rosalind had no alibi, but the story she told and the information they had collected pointed to her innocence. The Dijon girl, on the other hand, most assuredly was involved. There was nothing concrete yet in the way of evidence, but given what she had been all these years, could anyone doubt that she had played a part in Colsey's death? Given her impetuous nature, moreover, her strength and size, could anyone question her leadership of the group that killed him? She was the only one with a motive. He had attacked her sexually before. When he tried again, she bludgeoned him to death. Probably she would have done it with her bare hands too, except she knew that would leave marks on her hands and the body, which would make it easy for the police to trace her.

For eleven months, as she awaited trial, Bobbie Dijon

steadfastly denied knowledge of the crime. She had been "messing around" with her friends that Sunday, and if the police chose not to believe her or her friends, that was their business. When the trial began she would be assigned a lawyer, for the little good she believed that would do.

"Why should a lawyer believe me any more than the police do?" she erupted every time the subject of a legal representative arose. "Nobody helps the down and outs. All anybody does for us is build us nice little jails where we can go and have a wonderful time. All of us would rather be in here than out walking on those dirty dangerous streets. I mean, little kids like me, we could get hurt out there. We'd much rather be in here where it's nice and warm and they give us wonderful things to eat, not only three times a day, but every time we get hungry. All you have to do, you know, is ring for the maid or the butler and tell them what you want and they bring it to you. You don't even have to pay. The state, the blessed state, pays all your bills. You just say, 'Charge it,' when the maid comes. 'Course sometimes they make you make your own bed, but you know, that's just the price you have to pay for being in this beautiful resort. You really should try it. It's really so nice in here, I don't understand why anybody would want to stay on the outside. I mean, it's nothing compared to this. 'Course it isn't the nicest spot in the world if you mind getting raped or having your teeth kicked out once in a while."

Bobbie Dijon never actually recorded her experiences in jail, but to those interested in hearing her accounts of it, she told remarkably detailed stories. When no one came to visit her, she told herself the day's events. She was storing them in her mind, hoping that one day her mother or her real father would be eager not only to hear about them, but to side with her in her defense.

When she was first locked in her cell, she became violently ill. She felt her head getting warm as if the blood in her neck were being heated and rising hot into her brain. Then she felt as though her head was suddenly too heavy for her body to support. Her heart raced and perspiration appeared all over her body. She vomited violently, surprised that there had been no warning signs of nausea or abdominal pressure. Her fingers and toes tingled as though someone were sticking needles into them, and she was afraid that she was losing her sense of touch. Her eyesight too was affected; images became blurred and a strange scintillating arc appeared above everything she focused on, giving the impression of electrical interference.

"I'd never been sick before. Little stuff maybe, but not like that. I remember sitting on the bed looking at my own vomit. I couldn't believe I'd vomited. It didn't feel like I'd done it. I couldn't smell it neither. Like, when they put me in the cell it didn't feel like me at all. I know I was there, but it didn't feel like me. I had to keep telling myself, it's really happening. But I know how sick I was and like, I can't say I really love my old lady, but when I got sick I really wanted her. I was calling for her and everybody was telling me to shut up. I must have been calling too loud. I was begging for her to come and take care of me. That's all I wanted. Sure, I wanted to get out of there and go home. Everybody thinks that all the time. But I wasn't thinking that so much then. All I wanted was my old lady to come and help me, take care of me.

"The thing is, I didn't know how sick I was or why I got sick 'cause I'd never been sick like that. I thought I was going blind or having a heart attack. If you never had those things happen to you, you don't know what's going on. But those people in the jail, they know what's going on 'cause they told me later that lots of girls get sick the same way I did. They know what's going on. But you think they helped me? Hell, no. This guard, the matron, she walked past my cell fifteen times while I was in there sick and crying. I didn't remember seeing her there 'til much later. You think she stopped to look at me? She didn't even slow down. Just walked right on past me. All they care about is whether you're in your cell like you're supposed to be. If you get sick in there they don't care. That ain't their problem. It's yours!

"I feel I'm getting sicker in here. Every day, just a little bit more. The place terrifies me. Sometimes I feel I'm screaming to get out, but it's all quiet. If a person's in prison 'cause he's done something, then he can't complain. Everyone in here says she's innocent. I don't think I've talked to more than a couple of women who say, 'Yeah, I did it and they caught me.' Everyone's always saying they're innocent. Like me. But they've all been through a trial and everything. And some of the trials went on and on and on. But me and Rosalind, we ain't never even had a trial. No one's proved nothing about us. They just said get in there until we set up a trial or something for you. I think that's why I'm getting sicker. I don't want to go mad. I fight against it, but it's like this large wall is moving in closer to me every day and I can't push it back anymore. There used to be a time when I thought I could, but not now. I don't know why it is either.

"I've been in this jail and another one for nine months! Nine months and one week. I went in on a Monday. Monday night. Like, the first couple of months I spent time getting used to the place—getting used to it, that's a laugh— and spending my time being angry 'cause they had no right keeping me in here. Then I started to change. Sometimes when you change you don't feel it happening. It just happens and one day you look back and say, I guess I've changed. But *this* time I really knew I was changing. Every day, twice a day, I would say, I'm not like me anymore. For a while I even stopped slouching over like I do. I wanted them to think they'd never break me. They got informers in here, you know. Ladies, maybe they're police, maybe they're real prisoners. They try to break you down, get you to confess things. One of them put a lighted cigarette on my ass one night. Honest to God, she held it closer and closer, they must have had six of them holding me down. She kept saying, 'I'll put a hole right in the middle of your goddam ass if you don't tell us what you did.' I always wondered how come the matrons let it go.

"This one inmate they got here, Roxanne something. Nobody knows her last name. They call her Roxanne the Plumber 'cause when you don't talk what they want to hear she shoves this metal snake up inside you. Nobody knows for sure what she is. I'm sure she's a cop 'cause nobody's ever seen her sleeping in her cell. And sometimes she'll disappear like for days. She *must* be a cop, although when we ask her where's she been she says they punished her for something. I think she's a cop. She just goes home. Can you believe that woman spends a couple hours a week in a woman's reformatory trying to get inmates to talk by burning them with cigarettes and ramming plumbing snakes they use to clean out sinks up their asses, and then goes home and cooks her old man's dinner? 'How'd it go today dear?' 'Not so bad, Honey. I crammed a few snakes up a few girls' assholes this afternoon but otherwise it was just a regular old day at the office.' Jesus, those kind of people are sicker than us.

"See what I mean by I can't take it much longer? I think about my parents too. I miss my mother a lot. She says she's trying to get out here once a week. Couple of times she came out twice. But then I'll go weeks and I won't see nobody. No letters, nothing. There's a girl in a cell near me who gets something in the mail every single day. Every day!

I don't get nothing ever! Maybe if I did it'd give me something to keep me from thinking I'm getting sicker. 'Cause you can get sick around here and nobody will come and take care of you. They used to get sick a lot. It was a way of getting somebody to talk to you. Now they don't believe you when you get sick. That time I was vomiting? They said I was faking. I told them to smell it if they thought it was a fake. They said that the vomit was real but I was sticking my finger down my throat to make myself vomit. You believe that? Can you see me having this conversation with a matron about whether or not I vomit 'cause I really have to or 'cause I'm sticking my finger down my throat so I can get a little attention? It's ridiculous. It's like that time in court when all these big shots were talking about the murder of that slob, Ben Colsey, and all I could think about was how stupid a name Arnold is. My mind does the same thing when I talk to them about vomiting. I'm arguing. I'm crying most of the time too, feeling sorry for myself like an old dog. But inside my head I'm saying. 'Boy this is terrific. I don't have to be in school anymore talking about mathematics or the Middle Ages or the Crusades which I don't really understand. Now I get to talk to a matron, a real live woman who gets paid by the state, about vomiting. I'll bet a lot of taxpayers would love to know where their money goes.'

"Well, Mr. and Mrs. Taxpayer, you've probably been wondering about prison reform—that's what they call it—and you've probably asked yourself, now what do they mean by prison reform? Well, I'll tell you. In the old days in our quaint little ladies prison when one of the prisoners got ill—say she began vomiting during the night—we would train our little matrons to run in there, right into the cell at any hour of the day or night and help that prisoner. We might even take them to the prison hospital. But now we dont' do that anymore because we have prison reform. Now we train our guards to argue with the prisoner about whether or not they're vomiting because they're sick, or just gagging themselves because after three weeks of not doing anything or talking to anybody they seem to need a little attention.

"I think I'm going crazy. I think they're *making* me go crazy. I think they're killing my body first, that's what I mean by the wall coming in on me, then I think they'll start working on my mind. That'll be the next wall moving in on me. They'll do that pretty soon too because they don't want me to go to court and find out I'm really innocent like they know I am and that they've locked me up for so long when they had no right to do it. That's why they're doing this. They'll roll me into the courtroom and I'll be blabbering like a fool. A tall fool. So even if the judge says he can't tell whether I murdered Colsey or not, he's got every reason in the world to think I'm insane and should be put away anyway. It's like the cops used to tell me, 'It's only a matter of time before we get you.' I'm getting to think it really is only a matter of time."

Three weeks before she was to be called to trial, Bobbie Dijon was found dead in her cell. She had swallowed more than a bottle of sleeping pills that she had asked a fellow prisoner to get for her. One rumor went that her brother Timmy knew about her plan to commit suicide but promised Bobbie he would never say anything. Timmy Dijon denied knowing anything of his sister's plan. Marianne Dijon did not cry upon hearing the news of her daughter's death. Her body grew stiff and she whispered, "I knew it would come."

The police have never solved the murder of Benjamin Colsey, although they remain convinced that Bobbie Dijon played a role in it. Rosalind Warkovsky, who was released on her own recognizance following a hearing, claims she is certain Bobbie knew nothing about Ben Colsey's murder until the police picked them up on that cold Sunday night.

Six months after Bobbie Dijon's death, Patsy Monahan received a letter from a man named Stuart Post who claimed to be Bobbie's father. The letter showed no return address. It contained a twenty-dollar bill and a note saying the money was to be given to Bobbie to use any way she wanted. She was to know it had come from her father. Marianne Dijon denied ever knowing anyone by the name of Stuart Post. "Besides," she added, "it's all too late for that."

2

I'm Crying 'Cause They Took Away My Future

Sara Hoover moves slower now since her heart attack. Not so many years ago she was the most active woman in all the West End, but then came that fatal night in early April, the night of the crippling snowstorm that hit the city just when everybody believed spring had come. Sara Hoover had been trudging through the snow on her way home from work. The cold and wind were so intense there was no way people could protect themselves. Many sat in their cars waiting for something magical to happen. People with money checked into downtown hotels and telephoned their families to say they would try again to reach their homes tomorrow. People without money had no choice but to try to reach their apartments, which in Sara's case was ten blocks from the bus stop.

Suddenly she was overcome with intense pain in her chest and an inability to catch her breath, as if someone were pressing a foot down on her abdomen. In the middle of this freezing cold night she found herself perspiring, partly from the attack, partly from her fright, although she knew what was happening. Her brother Charles had died of a heart attack two years before and had described his symptoms in vivid detail. He had told Sara that heart problems ran in their family and that she had better start taking it easy, especially in the winter. She had said that people working two jobs don't take it easy, not in the cold weather, or the hot weather either. Then there was her son Fernall who would give any mother a heart attack the way he got himself in trouble with the police. Charles predicted that Sara, even though she was only forty-eight, would be struck down like he had been, but even he would have been surprised that her attack came so soon.

How she managed to make it home in the snow no one, not even she, can explain. And why she didn't die on the way to or at the hospital where the next morning her daughter told her that Fernall had again been picked up by the police, no one understands. She did survive the attack and the news of her son's most recent difficulty, but she was a changed person. Everyone noticed how slowly she walked after the attack. It wasn't out of fear that she might be stricken again; she simply could not get herself to move faster; the energy was gone. She looked older. The lines in her face were deeper, her hair seemed thinner, and gray-blue lines circled her eyes. Her voice too had changed. Whereas once she spoke in a pure, clear tone, her voice now was muted, thick, as though she should constantly be clearing her throat.

"It's a warning, probably the best thing that could have happened to you," her lone surviving brother McNall told her. "You been going too hard, letting that son of yours destroy you. Let's see how he takes to having a sick mother who can't fight him no more like she used to. *That* battle's over anyway, and it's a good thing. I say it's a damn good thing, maybe a sign from heaven. Lord didn't take you 'cause he didn't have to. Just scared us all a little. Now I want to see how that son of yours is going to act!"

It was true that Sara Hoover had fought bitterly and regularly with her son. At fifteen and a half, Fernall Hoover was one of the most handsome boys in his school. He wore his hair in a thick Afro. He had high, pronounced cheekbones, a sharp jaw, and a straight nose. His skin was smooth and each view of him seemed to effect a different appearance. It was as though he possessed several faces, each of them more interesting than the next. There was a deceiving quality about his appearance too, for at times he looked to be no more than twelve, while at other times he could pass for twenty. He used this to his advantage. When he got into trouble he turned on his little-boy look and played the innocent troublemaker, foolishly influenced by older boys. When there was a smart-looking eighteen-year-old girl, he would switch on his mature look and, as he said, "Impress the seams out of her."

Everyone knew the many faces and acts of Fernall Hoover. He was notorious for his roles, his lines, but his good looks and moments of innocence endeared him to people, even to some who could get rather angry with him. Between his looks and his charm, he just about had himself convinced he could squirm out of any difficulty, and there were many. "For a boy of his intelligence," one of his teachers said, "he sure can find the worst game in town, the worst boys to stay with, the worst of the dangerous stuff going around."

Sara Hoover claimed she knew from the beginning what sort of boy she had given birth to. Whenever someone would admire Fernall or, more likely, love him right out and say he had to be the most beautiful boy they had ever seen, Sara Hoover would brush the compliment aside: "Boy's too slippery for his own good. Boy's going to grow up thinking he can smile at people or move his head around so cute like he'll do and no one will get tough with him. He's going to learn. Someday he's going to learn. If his Uncle Charles or his Uncle McNall don't teach him with words then someone else is going to teach him with fists. He's too cagey for me. Don't trust him. Even though he's my blood I don't trust him. Just can't get myself to believe a word he tells me."

By the time he was ten, Fernall and his mother had begun a running battle. Not a week passed without them quarreling over something. Usually it would start with Fernall lying about something he had done, like going to the movies when he was supposed to be in school, or with Sara accusing him of lying. In the beginning it was bad words, with Sara occasionally slapping the boy's face when he used foul language which she forbade in her home. She also disapproved of Fernall blaming his trouble on someone else. "You take responsibility for yourself," Sara would demand of her son. "Don't you go blaming this one and that one. You do good things, you can take all the credit you like, just so your head don't get bigger than it is already. But when there's blame to be taken, then you stand up like a man and take it like a man."

"Ain't what *you* do," Fernall would sneer at her. "You blame Dad, don't you?"

"Shut your mouth about your father," Sara would reprimand him. "What I did with your father ain't no business of yours."

"Oh no," Fernall would say sarcastically. "No business at all. Just my father. Just left here and won't ever come back in this home 'cause you treat him like dirt. That's all. But it ain't *my* business."

It was true that Sara Hoover had made life hard for her

estranged husband Roy Edward. Then again, he had been tough with her, or so it seemed to their four children who wanted to be certain their father was properly represented in arguments. Actually, Fernall had reconciled himself to visiting his father whenever he could. He would have preferred to have his father at home, but when he thought about the explosions that resulted from his parents being together, he knew it was best that they live apart. Throughout his childhood he had heard them fight. Each accused the other of stealing money from their savings, each accused the other of drinking and of making life unbearable for the children. They separated when Fernall, the youngest, was three, but they never were officially divorced. Sara said she wanted a divorce but Roy Edward "wanted to keep the back door open."

"You never know with a man like that when he'll choose to reform himself and come home. That's where Fernall learned all his lying and deceiving from, from his father. Saying one thing one moment, another thing different the next. The two of them deserve each other. One minute he wants a divorce, final, complete. Next minute he says maybe we should wait. You think I saw him when I had my heart attack? Hell, no! Not a word. Not a letter from him, and he knew how to reach me. No, he played it cozy. Soon as I got better then he comes around one afternoon seeing whether he can't borrow a little money from me. Says he got some business deal he's preparing with his friends. They're going buying booze, that's all it is. Trust a twelve-dollar bill 'fore I'd trust that man with a nickel. Fernall knows how I feel. He wants to see his father, that's his business. Let 'em talk about how well each of them is doing and what a rotten old lady I am. Go ahead. They're one and the same."

Sara Hoover knew that neither she nor Roy Edward would ever remarry. It wasn't that they were too old, both of them being less than fifty. They had made an attachment to each other that neither would ever cut off. Sara believed that if she died prematurely, Roy Edward would remain a widower to the end of his days. She made certain that Fernall believed this as well, although the boy talked to both his parents about getting remarried. They told him it was too expensive and too late, but he insisted they had lots of time left to enjoy life. They would look at him as if to say, "We tried it once, that's enough." Getting remarried is for other people. He knew that with all the battles he had witnessed as a child, there was still a feeling of love between his parents. His two brothers and sisters saw it too, and the presence of it bewildered them. Each of them said they would have preferred their parents either getting back together or settling on a final divorce arrangement. The in-between state they had maintained for twelve years was too straining.

It never took much for Fernall to throw all this at his mother when they got into one of their arguments. He didn't dare question his father's position and attitudes, so all of his frustration and anger erupted with his mother. When he was thirteen he was throwing temper tantrums in front of her. No sooner had the argument started than Fernall would push over tables and hurl chairs and dishes about the small apartment. He was always careful not to hurt his mother, but he could barely control his desire to hit her. He restrained himself during her period of recuperation following the heart attack, but in a few months the vicious battles were being waged all over again. When Sara would warn her son that she might keel over at any minute, he would only yell louder and accuse her of using her illness to get her way.

"Go to hell, Pretty Boy!" Sara shouted at him one afternoon when she couldn't take his temper anymore. "Take your father too. You want me dead, I'll die. You want me out of your way, I'm as good as gone already."

Fernall couldn't believe his mother calling him Pretty Boy. He had always thought his mother loved him partly for his looks, but he couldn't tolerate her deriding him. He stormed into the kitchen and pulled the refrigerator down on its face and left the apartment.

Even as a small boy Fernall Hoover knew young men in his neighborhood who were getting into criminal activities. He used to sit with them when they talked about stealing watches or "bumping off" people on the subways, by which they meant purse snatching. By ten he belonged to a loosely organized group of boys who spent their days cutting school and stealing. The group could make upwards of one hundred dollars a week. They used Fernall as a lookout or a carrier of stolen property. He would accompany an older boy who, after stealing something, would give it to Fernall and disappear. The police never suspected the little boy with the lovely face. And Fernall would look up at everyone with his big eyes and gorgeous smile as though wondering how these people could ever presume he would know anybody who would snatch a wallet. He was merely waiting for his mother to pick him up, he would answer when they asked what he was doing in the city's main hotel district on a school day. He had a doctor's appointment and she was coming to meet him. Fernall would pull out a piece of paper with a note from his mother explaining why he was downtown, a note one of the older boys had written, and off he'd walk, looking back over his shoulder at them with that lovely face of his and the expression of, "I don't know what you all take me for." Inside his shirt and underwear he would be carrying perhaps fifty dollars in cash and twenty credit cards.

"I was scared then too," Fernall remembered. "I don't know what I was doing. It was like I was hiding behind my face. I wasn't telling myself what to do, or what I wanted to do. It was all these other people. They told me what to do and what to say. I wasn't doing anything myself, except being scared, I suppose. Even with girls. When I was ten I went out with this girl who was maybe fourteen or fifteen. She knew I was younger but she didn't know how young. But I had this older guy named Felix something. He told me what to do with her, so I did it. She even said I was pretty good. All I knew was I was scared. I was always scared. But they were pushing me around like I was a little doll or a puppet, you know what I mean. I knew it was happening, but I always told myself, when you're small you got to listen to people, that's the way you learn. You don't read books about *everything*.

"Most kids learn a lot from their folks, but we learned you don't learn anything from them. I wanted to talk to my father, but either he was never around, or when I'd go and see him he'd be drunk or too busy to talk to me. Or sometimes, he'd want to tell me about what was going on in *his* life. He thought he was doing me some kind of favor telling me all these things, but I didn't go to his place to talk about *him;* I went there to talk about *me!* He never seemed to catch on to that. He was too busy being interested in himself. It was like he'd forget I was his son. He'd act a lot like I was his brother or his business partner or something. So I'd get mad, only I wouldn't show it. If I got angry with him like I did with my old lady he'd have punched me in the head 'til I never talked to no one again. I couldn't get angry with him. So I'd listen 'til I could tell he was tired of talking with me, then we'd go out and he'd take me to a bar where he knew lots of people and start acting like he was someone important, you know, like down at this one place called Sweets. 'Hiya Johnny, hiya Billy.' Like he was somebody famous. He only did it to impress me. I always knew he was nothing, that he didn't have nothing. Hell, he didn't even have the strength to divorce my old lady. Didn't have a job half the time, I know *that* for a fact. Couldn't hold one. He's got the same mean temper I do. Neither one of us could ever amount to much. He knew that. So did I. That's possibly how come we always talked to one another without really talking to one another, if you see what I mean.

"He knew I'd end up in prison. I knew I would too. There wasn't much that either one of us could say. Certainly wasn't going to be anything anyone could do to stop it from coming down. I could see where I'd end up when I was ten years old, scouting for those kids, snatching old ladies' bags in the Clifford Street station. You got to end up in prison. Every cop in the city gets to know you by the time you're eleven or twelve. They sure as hell knew who I was. Hell, I was starting to know *their* names I saw them so often.

"Maybe what a kid like me thinks is the best place for him is prison, 'cept you don't know what prison is like 'til you've been in it. I mean, *I* didn't know. All I knew was what I saw on television. It didn't look so bad on the tube, but no one can tell you how it's going to be. But like I say, maybe I needed to be in 'cause they do protect you in here, and they do something else too, they, like, keep you controlled, behaved. Like, when your head is saying go rip off some sucker, you know you can't do it in prison unless you go after one of the dudes in here and he's likely to kill you 'fore he'd let you rip off something as small as a match. It's like they got your arms tied behind you even when they don't have you at all. But it ain't all that bad, feeling you ain't suddenly going to break loose, lose your temper, throw over the furniture like I used to do with my old lady.

"I don't get too many of those tantrums or whatever you'd call them in someone my age in here. Man, I could just be looking at my old lady and hear those words coming out of her mouth before she even said them and I'd be set to flip a table over on her. That time I pushed the refrigerator down? Hell, I was angry with her that time two hours 'fore she even came home. That's true. I was just sitting there in my room on one of the days I cut school—couldn't take that school gig either. But that one time with old Sara, hell, I was sitting there for hours on my bed, doing nothing, man. Nothing but thinking. Had my mind racing all over the place; I don't know what I was thinking. I mean, I couldn't tell nobody what I was thinking about if they asked me. Maybe something about my father 'cause I'm always thinking about him. Then I remember my legs jumping up and down like I was some race car with nowhere to go, probably 'cause of what I was thinking about my father. But that don't happen too much in jail, only once in a while. I think all the stuff I always thought, but I know I could go crazy and never leave the cell. With my mother all I had to do was hear her coming up the stairs—I didn't even see her, man, just heard her footsteps climbing up those stairs like they were saying. 'I'm old and I work too hard and nobody helps me, 'specially Fernall,' you know, 'so I'll probably die before I make it to the top.' I was ready, man, to pound the life out of her by the time she unlocked the door. She's lucky all I did that one time was pull the refrigerator over on the floor. Didn't even break nothing either. Never had much food in it anyway. Fact I never could see why we even bought it in the first place. What's the sense of having a new refrigerator if you don't have money to buy food to put in it? Never made no sense to me. I used to ask Sara about it.

" 'What'd you get it for if you never use it? Just so you can tell people we got so much money lying around we went out and bought a new refrigerator?' 'That's what you want to believe,' she'd say, 'then you go right on believing it.' 'I don't want to believe nothin', Sara,' I'd go. 'All I want is to come home from school one day like every other kid in this country, come home, you know, a little hungry 'cause what they give us to eat in school ain't **half** as good as what they throw away in this prison, and go in that nice old white refrigerator and find a little *snack*. You know what I mean, Mamma? A nice little *snack*. But all I find in that refrigerator is soap and some wet towels and a bottle of milk that's so old you can't even smell it much less drink it and a loaf of bread so rotten it's turning green, and it's got this gray, fuzzy crud growing on it.' Lots of folks, you know, they get so hungry they eat bread like that. They know they might get sick from it, but they wipe it off and eat it. I wouldn't go near bread like that. I told that to her too. 'How come I come home from school and all you got is bread in that refrigerator with that gray, fuzzy crud growing on it? Least you could do is throw the damn stuff away where no one's going to eat it, 'cause a baby would eat it, you know. Baby don't know the difference between good bread and bad bread.'

"So you know what my old Sara says to me? She says, 'Fernall, the problem with you is that when you ain't complaining, you're lying. Poor little boy coming home from school and he don't find what he likes in the refrigerator. Boy, you're a *liar!* You're coming home hungry all right, but you ain't coming home from school. You ain't been in school for weeks. Weeks you ain't been there. You think I don't know? You got no complaints about nothing. You want fresh bread and milk in that refrigerator then go out and get yourself a paying job since school ain't taking up your time no more, and buy food and stick it in there. Then you just put a little label on each thing you buy and write your name on it. That is, if you know how to write your name. Your *gang* teach you that or they too busy teaching you what to do to get yourself thrown in prison?'

" 'You *want* me in prison, Sara,' I yelled at her that one time. 'You want me and Roy Edward and probably every other man you ever knew rotting in prison just like the bread you keep in that refrigerator. And don't tell me it ain't true neither, or are you going to do your number about you're dying of a heart attack and it's all my fault. Maybe you're going to tell me for the five hundredth time what Uncle Charles told you. Don't let 'em do it to you, Sara. They'll kill you off, Sara. Get rid of that boy, Sara. Get rid of him 'fore he kills you off. My children did it to me, Sara, your children going to do it to you. Best thing for that boy, Sara, is for him to be in a prison. Any prison. How young they taking these boys nowadays? I tell you, Sara, it'd be the best thing that ever happened to you, best thing happened to the family as a whole since you got rid of Roy Edward. Get 'em out of your life, Sara. Every year they're gone, that's just another year you're walking about on the earth, no matter how bad it is for folks like us.'

"My mother heard those words she practically threw the refrigerator at me. Neither of us could control ourselves. Both of us needed to be in some kind of jail most likely, but it had to be one of us. I suppose it was right it had to be me. I mean, I don't love it in here or nothing, but I ain't got a whole helluva lot waiting for me when I get out. I'll get out in a while, sooner or later, don't make that much difference to me the way I feel about it now. Then I'll be out there looking for a job and I won't find one, or maybe I'll get one and lose it and get another. I'm only assuming all this 'cause the world don't pile up jobs for kids like me with records. There aren't that many jobs around for nobody, especially folks in my category. Anyway, I'll be back in here, someday. Has to happen. I'll need money out there, right? Where'm I going to find it? Lying in the middle of the street? My dad going to give me something? He ain't got enough to live himself. He's always taking it from my mother and she always took it from my Uncle Charles, 'til he died. I don't know where she gets the money she needs now. So, you fall in with some dudes like me. Some got records, some going to get them in a matter of weeks or months. Don't make no difference. Cats don't necessarily love one another, just need each other, that's all. Need each other to survive. Everybody's like soldiers, if you see what I mean. So I'll be back."

Fernall Hoover appeared in court four times before he was sentenced to three to five years for breaking and entering and carrying a gun, albeit one that was not loaded. He was fifteen and a half. The judge was getting tired of seeing Fernall coming in and going out of court. "It is almost amusing to think," the judge said, "that you might be in here more days a year than you're in school. You could have a future. You've got brains and you've got charm, and those two things could serve you well. But somehow, you have a need to spoil everything you touch. Why in God's name every time you make a simple decision in your life you choose the option that *has* to lead to the greatest risk and the greatest trouble is beyond me. Maybe somewhere in your mind you really *want* to go to prison. But that's not the reason I'm sending you there. It's because of a woman named Sara Hoover. I take it you've heard of her. We have witnesses, not only police, who swear that you and your mother have violent fights, not just once in a while but all the time. I also happen to know that your mother has been seriously ill and needs to be disturbed as little as possible. And since you seem to be the biggest disturbance in her life, maybe in the short run *and* long run it is better for you to go somewhere and get out from under her feet. Maybe you need to cool off for a while. What do *you* think about it?

Fernall could say nothing. Two days later he began his prison term.

During his two and a half years in jail, Fernall Hoover was placed in solitary confinement on three occasions, the first time when he was sixteen. He had been fighting with another inmate and when a guard attempted to pull them apart he became incensed and hit the guard and everybody else who tried to hold him down.

His descriptions of his prison experiences are always told in the same placid manner, his voice rarely rising or falling. A naive observer might believe he forgets each day in jail as soon as it passes, but it is obvious that rage and hurt lie close below the surface of his even manner. He has been strangled in prison, especially by the experience of solitary confinement in an eight foot by eight foot cell for days at a time.

"First thing I realized, man, I didn't know the time. Room had no windows so I never could tell. Sometimes, you know, when you ain't sleeping you can sort of tell how many minutes passed you by. But when you're sleeping, you don't know. Ain't got no clock, ain't got no sounds to help you. You're in a cell. First I thought, I can dig it, they bring me my food, I'll make out, you know what I'm saying? But after a while they got you talking to yourself. I'd be standing in there yelling loud as I could, 'Tell me the time. *Tell me the time.*' Ain't no one going to answer you. You know that, but it don't stop you. You just keep on yelling, '*Tell me the time. Is it the day or the night?*'

"Pretty soon, man, I figure I'm going crazy. I ain't even seen where I am. Suddenly the whole cell gets real light, you know, and I'm blinking my eyes so's I can get used to it. Then when I open 'em I can't see nothing. It's still black in there, 'cause I only *imagined* they turned the lights on. Then I start talking to myself, 'You ain't going crazy, man. You're doing all right. You're going to be all right. Believe me, you're going to be all right. Just hang in there.' So I tell myself, 'Think about the future, man, think about how it's going to be for you when you get out. Make it like a picture in your mind,' you know what I mean.

"So I start to imagine the future, man, and there's nothing there. I can't see nothing, man. It's like a cell, all dark and nothing there, nowhere to go, nothing to see. Could be something there but if it is I'll be goddamed if I can see it. So I'm crying in there, man, like I was this little boy or something. I'm really crying. I ain't shitting you. I'm crying 'cause I ain't got no future. I'm like my little brother used to get when we'd take away his toy or this blanket he carried around with him everywhere. Sitting on the floor crying so loud, you know, no one could shut him up. I'm crying 'cause they took away my future. I try to pull myself together, man. I say, 'Okay, man, hold on, pull yourself together. Forget about this long future, this rest of your life stuff. You just be calm now, stop crying and start thinking about tomorrow.' That's how I'm talking to myself. Just like that. So I try to settle down. 'Forget the future,' I say to myself. 'Just tomorrow.' Then, man, like it started raining or something, I'm crying all over again. Sitting there crying like my brother. You know why? You know why I'm crying? I'm crying, man, 'cause I can't think about tomorrow because I don't know when tomorrow's coming. I don't know when the day I'm living in is over.

"I went crazy in that solitary confinement thing, man. Before then, I knew I could get myself into a state that was really crazy. The sanest I ever was was when I was doing crime or doing drugs, you know. But the craziest was fighting with my mother, when everything just went berserk, or *trying* to talk with my father when I knew what I wanted to do was pull the furniture over, like the refrigerator, only he doesn't have one. But that first night in solitary, man, that has to be the worst night in my whole life.

"If anybody ever asked me to talk to a group of kids about getting into crime, you know, and going through the courts—which is a lot of crap 'cause nobody knows what anybody's doing there—and then getting sent to prison, I'd say prison is bad but you can make it if you keep your head. And if *I* can keep my head then anybody can keep theirs. But don't do nothing that's going to end with you being

locked up in solitary confinement. That has got to be the
worst trip in the world, man. I thought lots of times when I
was in there I was becoming somebody else, changing
persons you know, so when they'd let me out I wouldn't be
no one no more. I don't know who I thought I'd be, but it
wasn't going to be me, I can tell you. Talk about having
your head turned around, they had mine bent off so's it
practically fell off in their laps. Had my brains pouring out of
my eyes and ears is how it felt. Things spinning around and
staying the same and still at the same time. Seeing things
that weren't there—everybody says that about solitary. I
thought maybe they put something in my food, like some
drug. There's lots of talk about guys getting drugged with
things in their food. All of a sudden in the middle of the
night you see some guy freak out, right in front of you.
One minute he's perfectly all right, minding his business.
Next minute he's a goddam loony, running around, smash-
ing his head into a wall. Usually it's one of those quiet guys
too, somebody you don't notice. Then wham, he's going
crazy, pushing at everybody or trying to bite his way
through the bars. One guy they had here broke all his teeth
doing it. Hell, I bit so hard on my own hand that first time
in solitary they thought they might have to sew it up. And
all I was trying to do was keep myself from going more
crazy than I knew I was already.

"But see, here's something they never asked me about.
Anybody who comes in here learns plenty fast who to stay
away from and what to stay away from. What to stay away
from means solitary. That's number one for the younger
guys like me. Nobody *wants* to get sent there. They got
guards in here who love to drag guys over there, but most
of 'em don't want to. They know how it is. They'll threaten
us with it but everybody knows they don't want to do it.
But they never asked me how come I had that fight with
Dennison the night they put me in there. Nobody asked

what started it. They saw us fighting and they knew *he* didn't fight a lot and they got me pegged as the cat with the tantrums even though I behave all right in here. But they didn't ask. 'Course Dennison told 'em afterward but it was too late then. They put us both in solitary so they didn't find out 'til later. He got the letter saying my mother died and said he'd give it to me. All the letters are opened anyway so he read it. He got so upset so he kept it 'til that night. He was just frightened. They should never have given it to him in the first place. So I read it and went crazy, like I do. Like I always did with Sara. But hell, it's only normal to go a little off the deep end when your mother dies, especially when you're in jail and you know you never did too much in your life to help her get any better. So, I don't know."

3

Get Me Spiro Agnew's Lawyer

Robert Martin Gumpert was arrested for burglary. The arrest occurred one week before his fifteenth birthday. Gumpy, as he is called, is a white boy of medium height for his age, and very thin. He wears his hair long, usually hiding it under a cap. His eyes are a pale green and grayness often shows on his upper lids. His teeth have yellowed from years of neglect—he has not visited a dentist since he was seven—and an obstruction in his nose makes breathing difficult. When he speaks it always sounds as if he has a cold.

Gumpy was arrested with two other young men. After the arraignment and the completion of legal negotiations, he was placed in a county jail for what was supposed to be a maximum ten-day period prior to his scheduled appearance before a judge. Because the arresting officers listed Gumpy as being an accessory to the burglary, his case was considered less severe than those of the two other young men arrested with him, Manny Malzone and Frederic Fritz Gallaher. All three boys were placed in the same jail but were kept from seeing one another. There was no bail set for any of the three. Both Manny and Fritz had prior police records; Gumpy, although he had once been picked up by the police, had never been booked or fingerprinted. Ever since the neighborhood police had first gotten to know about him when he was nine, Gumpy was considered a loud-mouth troublemaker, but not a boy one would consider a criminal. It was always said that he was a follower. If his friends stayed clean, he would stay clean. If his friends decided to break the law, he'd go along with that too.

Bobby Gumpert sat in jail over a week awaiting trial. On the morning of the tenth day he learned that because of a judge's illness, his case would be continued indefinitely, but presumably no more than two weeks. He was still not allowed to be released on bail. In fact he waited forty-one days before trial, one of fifteen young men under the age of eighteen in a jail of about sixty-five prisoners.

During the forty-one days of his confinement prior to trial, I was allowed to visit once a week with Bobby Gumpert, a boy I have known for seven years. His mother, brothers, and sisters were allowed three visits a week, but because they lived so far from the jail they visited only once a week. My conversations with the boy were always the same. He was bewildered, angry at the treatment he was getting, and scared. As the days wore on, his terror and outrage increased. Several days before his trial took place—although at the time he did not know that a date had been set—we met in the visiting room of the jail for the last time.

"Do me one favor," he ordered me when he sat down.

"Promise one favor. Get me out of here. They're driving me crazy in here, man. They got guys locked up in here, man, who shouldn't be in here. I mean, nobody should be in here but these guys are off the wall, man. They're off the wall. They ought to be in a hospital. All night long I hear 'em talking to each other. They're whispering shit back and forth, man, they don't even make any sense. They're just talking. You can't believe it. There are old guys too. Guys in their forties, fifties, sixties. Jesus, I haven't seen another kid my age in there. Where the hell they sending all the juveniles anyway? There's only men in there. Everybody calls me Son. Hey, Son, do this. Son, do that. It gives me the creeps, man. They're going to drive me crazy.

"They got this one guy in there, he really thinks I *am* his son. Something happened to the guy's real son, I think. Maybe he was in a car accident or something. Somebody said he was electrocuted on the train tracks. Anyway, the first week I was here he decided I was his son. So he keeps yelling at me. Jesus, he gets me with this thing about me being his son. I'm a turn-on for him. So this other guy he says I ought to yell at him and shut him up, tell him I'm not his son, you know, or walk past him one day and kick him in the nuts. I can't do that, man. I don't know the guy. I don't know what he's been through. I just want out of here. I don't want to make no trouble. I just want to be transferred. If I'm guilty and have to go to prison or someplace, you know, then let them send me with guys my age.

"They got queers in here, man. Lot of 'em. Guys must have been straight once but not now. At night, you know, everybody's in there slapping meat, yelling, whispering. Guy this morning started to come at me from the back. I looked around, man, I couldn't believe this guy. I expected maybe it was Malzone, who I haven't seen all this time. He's a whack, he'd do something like that too. But Malzone? Hell, it was this old guy, a short, little, ugly guy. He must have been seventy years old. And he was standing there holding on to himself looking up at me like I was some chick. I swear to God, man. This guy was ready to poke it in me. Like getting stiffed by your own goddam grandfather. Jesus, man, they got me in with these old geezers. I think that's why they want me here. I think it turns these guys on. They don't have no women coming to see them so they put some kids in there like me and keep pretending the trial gets pushed forward. I'll bet that's it, too, man. I'm the goddam whore for this jail. Shit, they'd all shove it into me if they had a chance. I told this guard the other day, he wanted me to get outside for exercise. I mean he's cool. I told him I'm staying in here. Only safe damn place in the city. They'll keep those fags unlocked in their cells. That's what I heard. So when the guard's not looking, you know, they go in and get it on with each other. I ain't never seen that but I heard they did. I'll bet they do too.

"This ain't no place for a kid, man. Shit, this ain't no place for anybody but an animal and I ain't no animal. I still like girls, man. I ain't ready yet to have no guard molesting me. You hear what I'm telling you? It's me, Gumpy. I can't believe this is happening. It's a fuckin' dream, you and I talking in this place. We're in a jail, man. I'm going back after I talk to you to sit in a goddam jail cell. I ain't even got no window in that room. I can't look anyplace, man. I just pray they'll let me sleep but I never felt so healthy. The food here stinks but I'm really healthy, man. I don't want to sleep, man. I mean, I want to sleep but I don't need no sleep."

Bobby looked over his shoulder and then leaned across the table toward me.

"You got to get me out of here. Can't you find out if there's a kid's prison someplace? There's got to be one, man. I don't care where it is. I'd rather be in with nine-year-old kids than have to go back in there with those guys. They're going to eat me up in there, man. Eat me up or have me jerking them off one by one. I ain't told no one else but my brother, but you know damn well each person has a breaking point. They're going to break me in there, man. There's no one in there to look out for me. One of these days, if I don't behave like they want me to, they'll turn me loose on 'em. I've heard the stories, man. You go in there at ten o'clock in the morning and by ten thirty you've heard every goddam story about every goddam guy who's ever been in there. Whitey Polansky, this one guy everybody talks about? They said he made it with every chick in the city. Then they got him on this rape charge, you know. So they put him in here, man. and the guy goes A.C. Goes mad, man, and starts raping everybody in sight. I'll bet there were lots of guys in there who dug it too. So then he goes after the guard, this new policeman, you know. So the cop takes it for a minute then turns around and clouts the guy. Foom. I don't even know if he died or what happened to him after that. Someone said they took him to the South and cut his nuts off. Some sheriff, they said, cut his nuts off and tied them in the guy's pocket so he couldn't get 'em out. You believe that, man? That's what I heard. Maybe it's a lot of bullshit, but that's what I heard. Everybody that's been in there long enough has stories like that too. Old-timers have the most. But I got some stories now too, which means I've been in there pretty long.

"I saw some guy walking through the halls last night. Guy next to me says he thought it was the sheriff. I never saw the man before. Could have been the sheriff, could have been the plumber for all I know. Little red-faced guy. Funny looking. He kept smiling. I'd smile too if I could walk out of here the way he does. I'd take this whole place if I could come and go like him. And like you. So the guy, this sheriff or whatever he was, he comes walking up to my cell. I can see from the way he's looking in at me that he's surprised somebody young is sitting in on the bed, you know. 'How you doing, Son?' he goes. So I goes, 'Terrific. I love it here.' So he goes, 'Cut the shit, what do you need?' So now *I'm* the one who's surprised. So I stand up and go over to where he's standing outside the cell, you know. And he knows that maybe I want to tell him something which I did, only I don't know what I wanted to say. 'You can talk,' he goes, 'nobody's listening but me.' And when he's talking he kind of nods at these guards and they walk away. I could see them but they couldn't hear. So I guess he must have been the sheriff, or some big shot.

" 'You got a lawyer?' he goes. I tell him 'Yeah, a shitty one I never see.' 'What's his name?' he goes. 'Mooney,' I goes. 'Arthur the bullshitter Mooney. Mooney like Money.' 'He helping you?' he goes. 'Helping me to stay here. Somebody must be doing something super,' I goes, 'I been here six weeks.' 'Bullshit,' he goes. 'You're just waiting trial.' 'Bullshit nothing, baby,' I go. 'You ask 'em. Ask the guards. Six weeks, almost.' The guy was really upset. He was really upset. You couldn't fake the way he looked. I've seen people, like that Mooney, pretend he's interested in what you're saying, but this guy wasn't faking. Oh, man, I was standing there so close to him. I could see his freckles, you know, and these funny hairs growing on his head. The cat was bald, you know. So then he puts his hand around the bar holding it, and I'm standing there wanting to touch it. Jesus, maybe I'm queerer than I thought. But I really had this thing just to touch him, like to have contact, you know what I mean? So he goes, 'What do you need?' And he's serious. I mean, I know if I say get me out that would be silly, but if I asked him for a steak or a different shirt or change cells to get away from the creeps, maybe he'd be able to get it for me.

"So I look at the guy and he's really looking serious. He ain't saying nothing, just looking at me, holding on to the bar. So I goes, 'You want to help me, man?' I smiled like I was real tough and I didn't want to be. I couldn't help myself, you know. And I goes, 'If you want to help me, man, get me Spiro Agnew's lawyer.' It was dumb, man. Real dumb. I felt like a goddam asshole. I mean, the guy wanted to help, so what do I do, I tell him to fuck off. He knew what I was doing too. He goes, 'I'll do my best for you.'

"I blew it, man. The second he let go of that bar—it was like he'd been holding it up—I knew I blew it. I got so mad. And he walked away. I sat down, man, like I was really tough. Big, tough kid, you know, and all of a sudden I was crying, and I ain't cried since I don't even know when. But I was crying, man, and I didn't give a rat's ass if the whole jail knew it. Until that man came up to that cell and held on to that bar the way he did, you know, 'til I saw his hand holding on to that bar, I didn't know how bad off I am, and how scared I am. And I really am scared now too, man. I'm so scared now I can taste it."

After forty-one days of confinement prior to trial, Robert Gumpert's case went to court. In the end the judge ruled that he was guilty but suspended his sentence.

4

Nobody's Got Family Insurance

Elaine Harrington, sixteen years old, is a very thin, young woman with a look of defiance in her eyes. Every time one talks with her, one hears the same message: her wish to get even with somebody, her desire for revenge. For many years, there was only one person in her life that she actually believed was on her side, caring for her. That was her father, fifty-five-year-old Edward Harrington, an unemployed man who had worked for fifteen years in a coal processing plant. No matter what Elaine's difficulties she could always rely on her father. No matter how serious the problem he would be able to talk her out of trouble. Perhaps it would be a quiet chat with a policeman, or testifying before a judge on the two occasions when Elaine was taken to court. But whatever he said, it worked. She might get a whipping from her father after the ordeal was over, but that was preferable to going to jail. And besides, she always admitted she had it coming. Her father was a fair man; whatever he did was right.

Her mother, too, seemed reasonable and loving of Elaine, although it was sometimes difficult to know with Gloria Harrington. She had never been a happy person, one could see that on first meeting. Tall, attractive, a person interested in her appearance, and very quiet, she always looked as if she were about to weep. One always saw her blinking with exaggerated intensity as if fighting off tears. When she laughed, which she did only rarely, she seemed self-conscious, almost as if she were sinning. As she herself said, "No one approaching fifty who never had and never will have enough money and whose husband hasn't worked in years and may never work again can laugh anymore. I've had times to laugh. I had my days, even a few years now and again, although they were a long, long time ago. But no more. There's no more laughing going on in this home, not by me or anybody else. I feel foolish laughing. I feel like my entire body is being asked to deny everything going on all around me. I can't escape with television; we don't go to the movies anymore. We used to quite a lot when we first were married, and nobody escapes nothing by sitting down with the newspapers. And then there's *her*, my special daughter, who feels the greatest thrill in life is to break into somebody's car because it feels nice to sit behind the wheel of a car you'll never own. How's *that* for excitement. Fifteen years old, goes to school, reads her books, does her mathematics, tries to help me a little around the house— which is rare I'll tell you because this new crowd of youngsters we have coming up feel it's beneath them to do housework—and then for kicks, when she hasn't anything better to do, she goes with her friends and they find cars that aren't locked, or, when they're locked, they take that as a challenge to break in. I might even have a little more respect for them if they went all the way and broke in and stole the car. No way. Their big thing in life is to break into the car and sit there. Maybe they'll turn on the radio. You want to know what it is? In one word: They're nuts with a capital N!"

Gloria Harrington was pregnant with her first child when she was sixteen. On learning of the pregnancy, her parents disowned her. She suspected that Edward Harrington, the father of the child, would do the same thing. Instead, Edward promised to marry her when she got older and made arrangements for her to live with his Aunt Mary who had recently lost her husband and welcomed the company of another person in her empty two-room apartment. Aunt Mary moved her clothing out of the bedroom and let young Gloria move in. When the baby Anne-Marie was born, Mary proposed that Gloria let her care for the child during the day so that Gloria could return to school. But Gloria rejected the offer, preferring to care for Anne-Marie herself and rarely letting the baby out of her sight.

When Gloria was seventeen and a half, Edward made good on his promise and married her. In the beginning he moved in with his aunt but soon found an apartment for himself, his new wife, and his baby, who was then over a year old. In time there were six more pregnancies, four of the children surviving. It was discovered that Gloria had a rare blood cell anomaly which affected her pregnancies. Nonetheless, she and Edward were eventually the parents of five children, Elaine being the second to the youngest.

As was true for many of the young families the Harringtons knew, a simple and predictable series of events took place. Edward would be doing well in a job. His spirits were high and his relationship with his wife pleasant, if not always affable. It was said of Edward Harrington that he had women on the side. Surely he was a handsome enough man with a winning smile and a well-preserved body which he attended to assiduously. Gloria knew, or thought she knew, about the other women, although she could never prove anything. Yet deep down she felt she had no right to complain. Edward could easily have refused to marry her when she first got pregnant. In most every case she had heard of, the man left the woman to have the baby all by herself. Most of the boys in school who became fathers never even bothered to see their children, or, if they did, made life so difficult for everyone that the young mothers were glad to be rid of them. But Edward was different. He felt a profound obligation to Gloria and stayed by his word. When he was employed, he made a worthy husband and a helpful if not constant and relaxed father. When his job situation collapsed, he became scared and irritable. He moped around the house, shirking his few household obligations, and Gloria would realize it was only a matter of days before he would disappear on one of his binges, as she called them.

In the beginning it was true that Edward would go off somewhere and drink. He might pull himself together long enough to hunt for work, but after several hours in employment offices or waiting outside factories he would return to his favorite haunts with his special unemployed friends and drink himself into unconsciousness. Still, he always returned. After five days or a week he would suddenly be home, clean, freshly shaved, sober, begging his wife for forgiveness. And she always granted it. After all, Edward had married her, and, besides, where would a separation or divorce leave her.

It got harder, the scenes of fury and Edward disappearing then returning after several days. That the children gradually became implicated in the pattern didn't make it easier for anybody. Edward Junior seemed to be the most upset by the displays and periodic separations. He would grow angry when he realized his father was away. He would go into the room he shared with his brother Peter and start breaking things or pulling pages out of comic books and ripping the sheets off his bed. Gloria tried to be sympathetic but it grew more and more difficult to be civil in the presence of Edward Junior, because he was acting like a maniac. When she told him this, he would fly into a still greater rage and run out of the house screaming. Inevitably, Gloria imagined him storming out the entrance to the project apartment in which they lived and dashing in front of a car on Cedar Street, where there were never policemen to slow down the traffic. But Edward never did anything destructive. There were the occasional scratches and bumps, but he always returned, looking enervated, despairing, and dry-eyed, his own binge having run its fitful course. The next day he would rush home from school and wait on the top steps in the cold stairwell for his father. When it grew too dark to see the faces of the people trudging up the stairs, he went off by himself into the neighborhood, returning home after midnight, sleepy and hungry.

Often Gloria would prepare whatever bits of food she had and sit with her son while he ate, his coal-dark eyes telling her all his feelings, his anguish, his concern for and anger at his absent father. More likely, however, Gloria's capacity to tolerate not only her husband's reactions to unemployment but her children's responses to their father wore thin, and when young Edward came home, he found his mother furious. She would beat him with a belt, her fury intensifying when he refused to show any emotion even though she could see he was in serious pain. One night, almost taunting her, Edward entered the apartment and went immediately to the kitchen where he found a piece of bread. He yanked out his wide leather belt, threw it in the direction of his mother, then pulled down his pants and, still nibbling at the bread, shoved his buttocks toward her, inviting her punishment. Gloria swore at him, started to cry, then collected herself, grabbed the belt, and whipped him. In a few moments Edward too was crying.

Aroused by the noise, the other children wandered sleepily into the living room and through eyes that could barely focus, witnessed the spectacle of their half-naked brother being whipped by their mother. Peter vomited. Elaine giggled and called out to Edward, "If I were being whipped I'd at least have a peanut butter sandwich." With that, Gloria flung the belt at her, just missing her but knocking out a chink in the plaster wall. Elaine applauded, expressing her joy to such an excessive degree that even Edward looked at her with puzzlement. But in her anger and humiliation, Gloria Harrington could see that the look of defiance in Elaine's eyes, a look that surely was there when the child was born, was more pronounced than ever.

"I saw Elaine in that instant," Gloria would say years later, "and I saw all my life too. All her sadness and her being so hurt when my husband wasn't around, not that it is better when he's here. The children need him, I suppose, but not when he gets in one of his moods. The devil is the unemployment. It takes his pride away, his feeling of being useful to anybody, to us. The children know all about it. They probably understood it in their way when they were small. The Harrington pattern I call it. Anyone could see what was going on with us. Edward has a job, the family barely holds together. He loses a job, falls apart, Elaine gets that look in her eyes, it makes me so frightened I don't know what to do. Edward Junior goes crazy in his way, begging me, anybody I suppose, to beat him, hurt him, as if he was thinking things he shouldn't be thinking. God only knows, maybe he got into more trouble than any of us suspected when he ran out on his binges. And Peter being sick so much of the time, and the other two girls, like I didn't even know *who* they were much of the time when they were small. Funny too, because they were the ones that followed each of my miscarriages. I'd have a baby, then lose a baby, then have a baby, you know, and the two that followed the miscarriages, I must have treated them like they were fragile, like they were going to die or something. It was always like I was afraid to get to know them for fear I'd lose them. God only knows how they made out as well as they did, or maybe it's too early to tell.

"But Elaine, she knew when I'd look at her that I was thinking of myself as much as I was thinking of her. We never talked about it, I mean it's not exactly the sort of thing a mother talks about with a child, how you look at her and see yourself, your own life. Maybe it was because more than any of the children—none of them look alike, fact most people can't believe they're really brother and sister, which you can imagine how that makes me feel—but more than any of the others, Elaine looked like my own mother. Really, I should say, I *imagined* that she looked like my mother. If you compared photographs of the two of them, you might not be able to see the similarity. But *I* saw it. Funny, Elaine didn't always look like my mother, but when she was about four, almost five, I was taking the children to school one day, I guess I had little Edward, Elaine, Susan. Anne-Marie was going to a different school by then. Must have been early in the year when they were just starting. All of a sudden I said to myself, you know that Elaine looks exactly like my mother. Something in the way she turned her head or walked away from me into the classroom, like she didn't need me to stay with her—and she was only four, four and a half. It hit me then how much she looked like my mother. There's a lot of children who look like their grandmother or grandfather. Parents see that even when no one else can. Or maybe parents just want to believe their children look like their parents. But when I saw Elaine that one time I was surprised by how much they looked alike. But then I tried to imagine what my mother looked like. Like I tried to see her in my mind and I couldn't see anything. I couldn't imagine for the life of me what she looked like. I remember I didn't even have any recent pictures of my mother. And I had seen her too, fairly recently, although my father still refuses to see me and Edward and the kids. But I completely forgot what my mother looked like. I wonder what a psychiatrist would make of that."

Elaine Harrington never believed that her mother cared for her. She felt sorry for her mother for what had happened between her and her own mother, and she occasionally offered excuses for her mother's behavior. But she always believed that she had been an unwanted child, perhaps the child who was conceived in order to prevent a marriage from disintegrating. She always said that her mother preferred Anne-Marie and the boys and that she and Susan were seen as misfits. She said too that both her parents were convinced Edward Junior would become a hoodlum. Consciously, purposefully even, Elaine found ways to irritate her mother. She would stay out beyond her bedtime knowing full well that Gloria would be furious. Or she would promise to do something for her mother and then not do it. She would think about it but put it off until it was too late. Her mother would feel let down, personally insulted. Elaine drew no pleasure from this sort of behavior but it seemed as though she were driven to act this way by an inner source she could not control. When her father was working and the children seemed happy, she managed to find the strength to do things she knew would please her mother.

Once Elaine took some money she had saved from a job she held for three months and bought a small bouquet of jonquils for her mother. She came home with the flowers and put them in a little vase and left them on the dinner table without saying a word to anyone. When Gloria noticed them she was overjoyed and embraced her daughter. "Maybe this is just the beginning of a lot of good things for all of us," she cried. "And maybe we should continue the celebration with a little ice cream for dessert which is *my* surprise." That night the entire family went out to the Ice Cream Bath and bought double cones. They tasted each other's ice creams and enjoyed themselves as a family. Elaine was especially pleased, not only because her mother had responded spontaneously to the flowers, but that without being told, she had sensed that the flowers had come from Elaine.

Surely Gloria could have withstood the long periods of unhappiness had there been more evenings like this, but they rarely happened. Three months after the family celebration, Elaine Harrington was picked up by the police for car theft. It was the fourth time she had been taken to court. She was fifteen years old. On prior occasions her father had argued eloquently on her behalf. Elaine and her parents had appeared in court and followed the judge into private chambers where each time an arrangement of probation had been worked out. During one of these meetings the judge laid down a rule that Elaine had to be home by seven o'clock every night, weekends included, as well as check in with her probation officer once a week. The scheme worked for several weeks. Elaine came home immediately after school and asked permission to go out. But slowly her old ways returned and she stayed out later and later.

Another time the court put even stronger limitations on her activities but it proved no use—Elaine disobeyed and found ways of joining her friends. During her second probation period she was picked up for shoplifting, but the police, knowing her precarious status with the probation office, decided not to press charges. They learned too that Edward

Harrington was out of work, and jailing the Harrington girl would only add to the misery.

When two police officers found Elaine and Sheila Balinky in a long, blue station wagon owned by a suburban lawyer, the probation board decided it was time to put the girl away, and Elaine was brought into court. Since Elaine had been found in the driver's seat, she was accused of being responsible for the theft.

Two weeks after the trial, Elaine Harrington sat in the visitors' room of a women's prison and described her feelings in the courtroom, knowing that this time she would be sentenced.

"I wasn't warned or nothing. I knew my father would be able to do something like he always did in the past. He's a funny guy, my father. If he'd had any money when he was my age he'd have been a lawyer for sure. He's fantastic in there, defending me. The court gives you a lawyer but, I don't know, I suppose they do the best they can, but they don't really care that much what happens to you. They get paid no matter what the judge decides. But afterwards, my father always argues for me and he really influences them. He should have been a lawyer.

" 'Course this time he was really surprised by what I done. I guess I was too. We were drinking a little bit and I guess we didn't exactly know what we were doing. We were just walking, Sheila and me, and we saw this car with the windows wide open and the keys in it. Just sitting there. It was like the guy *wanted* us to steal his car or something. Maybe he wanted to collect a little insurance. Lots of people do that, you know. They get more for the insurance than they would if they traded in their car for a new one. Car was just sitting there, so we took it. We didn't take anything out of it, and he had a lot of stuff in there too, all his and his wife's tennis stuff, and a big suitcase which we didn't even open. All we did was take a drive. I mean, we weren't planning on taking the car or nothing. If you want to, you know, rip off a car like that and have it worked over in a body shop and drive it out the next day with new license plates, there isn't a cop in the business would ever be able to recognize that car was stolen. If you really wanted to steal a car, you wouldn't do what Sheila and me done. You wouldn't be sitting in front of a hamburger joint smoking cigarettes and talking like you were inviting the police to come over and arrest you.

"I counted on my father to get me off. I admit that. Maybe I even stole the car to get him to give me a little look, take care of me, you know. Families like mine, there's never enough time for people to take care of anybody. In some families, you know, when a kid gets sick, maybe his mother will stay with him at home, or in the hospital if he's really sick. But nobody ever knew what was going on with us, especially with me and Eddie. My mother's always sitting somewhere complaining about this or that or fighting with my brother and sisters, and my father's gone more than he's around, even when he doesn't have a job which means he really doesn't have no place to go. The only time I see him is in a courtroom or in the judge's chambers. That's the only time he's nice to me which is kind of strange too, isn't it? I mean, lots of kids you see coming here, they get bawled out by the judge then beat up by their parents. Me, they got the judge trying to do the best he can and my father showing the world how much he cares for me. Really weird. Sometimes, you know, I think I'd like him to punish me, not in front of all those people, but he should do *something*. The way it works now, it's almost like when I need a little loving from someone I go rip off a store or a car or something.

"No matter what else I do, nobody ever notices me. They

don't notice when I flunk a course, they don't notice when I pass a course. They don't care if I'm in school or cutting all my classes. Like they'll say, maybe, 'Elaine, did you go to school today?' 'Yeah, I went,' I say. That's all. They believe me. Like, I could disappear for a month and they'd say, 'Oh, hello, stranger. We ain't seen you 'round here for a long time. You been going to school?' 'Yeah, Ma, I've been in Brazil, but I went to school every day even though.' 'Okay, just so long as you go to school.' It's my father. He's the one everybody cares about. The whole family goes crazy when he's not around, not that we do so well when he *is* around.

"I think a lot about my getting into trouble. I always tell people it isn't fair what the cops or the courts try to do to me. But I don't know even what I mean. I mean, they're doing their job. What isn't fair is the way my father treats me and my mother and everybody. It's like I had to do something to call him from wherever he was. Like, he'd go off somewhere trying to kill himself 'cause he lost a job, which a lot of men do now, women too, and we'd always ask my mother, 'Where is he? *You* got to know. Someone has to know. His Aunt Mary knows where he is, so how come you don't?' And she'd say she didn't know but why'd we need him anyhow? He'd come back, he always did before. How come we needed him? Who the hell was she kidding? The whole house was falling apart without him there and she's asking why do we need him. For *you*, Mother. That's why *we* need him, for *you*. But she never knew from nothing. She didn't know where to find him which was the world's biggest lie because she did. You know how we knew that? Because if any one of us ever got into trouble, not with the police, but just little trouble, he'd pop right back into the picture. Magic, eh? A birdie told him. Or maybe he read about it in the paper 'cause we're all so famous. It's all bunko, baby. She knew. She knew all the time where he was. 'Cause when I got into trouble, magic, there he was, sober, dressed up in that brown suit of his—I always called it his court suit—all shaved, his hair combed. Didn't look too bad neither for a guy who hadn't worked in over a year or something.

"You know where he was all those times that Eddie and me and Anne-Marie got into trouble? Mother doesn't talk about Anne-Marie, I'll bet, because she wants to believe she did such a great job raising her. She's the one that was born before they got married so my mother keeps a special eye on her. She always thought if Anne-Marie turned out good and any one of the rest of us didn't, she could always say, 'You see the one I raised without the help of my great husband is the only sane one in the bunch. All the others are no good because he helped to raise them. Put in his little bit and ruined the whole lot of them.' My mother, see, she tells people that my father is this great guy, because he married her when he didn't have to just to be a good guy and a good father too, I guess. That's what she always says. But what she's thinking is that she has to prove to everybody that she really didn't need him. She could live with him or without him. Wouldn't make no difference to her. I honestly believe that too. I think she always wanted him to go away for good on one of his little binges. She goes mad when he's not there but I'm not so sure she doesn't like it better that way. But she knows where he goes and I know where he goes. You want to know where? He goes to Lorilee Marino's house on Shields and West Caledonian Road. Three twenty-one Shields; I've seen him go there. I've seen him with her lots of times.

"One night, you know, I was with some people and we went to this bar called Turpin's which is somewhere on the west side, but near Shields. I know *that* for sure. And the guy at the door, this big fat bouncer with red hair and this checkered vest looks at all of us deciding if we're old enough to go in there and drink. So my friend Nanny goes, 'Nobody ever stopped us here before.' 'Who's your friend?' the guy asks, and Nanny says some name so this cow in the vest goes, 'All right, you can go in but don't make no noise.' So we go in and it's dark in there. They got some music and we sit down. I've never been in the place before, you know, and all of us were wearing jeans and look ratty. But nobody says nothing to us. Then all of a sudden my friend Trish goes, 'Isn't that your father over there?' I goes, 'Where?' She goes, 'Over there in the corner, in that booth with the chick.' So I goes, 'No, that ain't my old man, you idiot. I don't know where my old man is but he ain't in here.' And it didn't look like him neither, best I could see, 'cause the place was so dingy, you know, and smoky and everything. But then I look again and it *is* him, and he *is* with this chick who I found out later was this Lorilee Marino or Cravino or something. So Trish is looking at me and I'm looking at my father and he's not only kissing the chick, I mean he's tonguing her to where I'm amazed she ain't gagging all over him and the booth and the floor and everything. I mean they're practically doing it right there in the booth.

"So Trish goes, 'It *is* your father, ain't it? I seen him. It's him, right?' I goes, 'No way. No way. Guy don't even look like him or nothing.' I'm lying and she knows I am, but she keeps quiet 'cause she seen how angry I am and how I'm practically crying. She never had anything like that happen in her life or nothing, but she could tell how much it was bothering me. And it really did too. Jesus, I'm lucky I didn't go out of that place that night looking for somebody to kill. It was like somebody took my heart away.

"You know why I got myself into trouble? Just to pull *him* away from that woman. I never knew if he knew I knew all about him. Maybe he did. I think he knew when I got into trouble, stupid kind of trouble that nobody with any brains would get into, that I was pulling him back to me and my mother. Then he had to fight for me because what I did, like get into some guy's car, wasn't half as bad as what he was doing. The rich man who owned that car, he had insurance. But nobody's got family insurance, where you collect money if somebody messes up your family, 'specially if it's one of your parents. He *had* to do good for me all those times, although he sure fell on his face this last time."

Elaine Harrington turned her head about, studying the visitors' room in the prison as though she were seeing it for the first time. Everywhere one looked young women prisoners were speaking to their families and friends, and yet there was almost no noise in the room.

"That pig, what'd he do for me when I needed it the most? All those other times he could do it, so what's he do the second they want to send me to jail. He cops out like you can't believe. Big shot with all his friends on the police force. That's what he told me. 'I got friends. I got friends.' That man don't have a friend in the whole world. He's a liar. He'd say anything to get you to like him. Showing off his teeth, that's all he does. His precious little daughter, what does he care if they take her to jail. Ain't no time out of *his* life, so what's he give a rat's ass about it for?

"I counted on him too. I believed him when he said he'd help. That lawyer they assigned to me, pile of hot air stuffed with shit. Second I looked at him I knew he couldn't do nothing for me. But I had my daddy, I said to myself. Good old reliable Daddy's going to pull me out of this. See if he don't. Well he *don't!* I don't know what the hell he did do but he didn't do nothing for me but bullshit everybody right down the line. They ought to stick him in here with them chicks and see how he likes it. He'd smell this air he'd see what a great thing he done for me."

Suddenly, Elaine Harrington's eyes were no longer filled with defiance but with penitence, and she was crying. She buried her face in her hands and shook her head from side to side, her long, black curls seeming to dance.

"Look what's happened. Look at all of us in here. This miserable goddam place has turned me away from my father. I *do* love him. I *do* love him. This place makes me say what I said. It's not *me* saying it. Honest it isn't. I *do* love him. I *do* love him."

5

Hey, Harrington, Put Your Pecker in Your
Pants, There's a Kid on the Phone Says He's
Your Son

In the beginning, it was true that Eddie Harrington ran out
of the house when his father disappeared on his binges and
sat by himself or took long walks. In the beginning, he could
not have been further from the boys in the neighborhood
who seemed to find trouble no matter where they went, or
what plans they made. He wanted no part of anybody. When
he thought he saw people he knew he would duck into an
alley or bolt across the empty lot near the project on Tyler
Street. And he would talk to himself.

"I'd tell myself, 'Okay, man. Get hold of yourself, don't let
yourself go all the way.' Stupid things like that. I couldn't
understand my dad just walking out on us. I didn't think I

was blaming him, because I didn't want to blame him. He's not a bad guy or anything. I knew he had a lot of problems. I guess I was always a little afraid of him, more than a little when he'd be fired from his job—he never admitted to anyone that he was fired but he was. Sometimes he was laid off, like a lot of men around here, but sometimes he was just fired. I was always hoping he'd come and talk with me. I was the oldest boy in the family and, you know, sometimes that happens. But he'd just go. I told him lots of times I'd like to go with him where he goes, but he said I had to stay around home 'cause I had school and stuff like that. Once he said, even if I cut school or quit for good—which he didn't want me to do—I could find better things to do than go with him. Honest, that's what he told me. I never told him nothing, but I was thinking that I'll never do anything that'll amount to all that much if I stay in school or quit this minute. I'm not meant to become much of anything. Never was either, even if things in my family or at school had been different."

In time, the running away to be by himself turned into running away and being consumed with fear. It was as if he were dreading the coming of a momentous event, a calamity even. Now he would hide in the corner of the project's small playfield as the afternoons grew dark, keeping an eye out for something unusual, a sign that the calamity was about to occur. In describing this new sense of dread, he once compared himself to a guard at the airport checking people's luggage to make certain no one was carrying a bomb. From his hiding places, he studied people's faces and memorized the shapes of buildings, counting the number of windows, and estimating the lengths and widths of door frames and fire escapes.

One night, on an occasion when his father had gone away, Eddie, who was then thirteen, collected a huge pile of newspapers and placed them in a dilapidated sandbox in the project playground, not far from one of the ground-floor apartments. Then he took some papers, rolled them up, and dipped them into the gas tank of a motorcycle he found parked two blocks away behind the supermarket. He recognized the cycle as belonging to Butchie Mayo, who worked as a checker at the market. After running through the streets with the newspaper smelling of gasoline, he reached the pile of papers in the sandbox. Carefully making certain that no one saw him, he set fire to the damp newspaper and threw it on the pile. In minutes a huge fire rose up from the sandbox. Suddenly people were running into the playground from their apartments and from the street. A woman leaned out the window of her kitchen and screamed for help. The fire was quickly put out by two men and the people who gathered near the sandbox returned to their homes wondering how it could have started. Eddie Harrington was never caught.

He repeated the action two weeks later. This time he could not find one reason for his behavior. His father was still out of work but had been showing up at home now and again. Eddie's school work was not that bad. There just seemed to be something pushing him to start a fire.

"I can't explain it," he would say later. "Sometimes things just come into my head, so I have to do them. Like, I'll be sitting on my bed, you know, and I won't be thinking anything special, but then suddenly I'm slamming my fist into the wall, really hurt it too. Only I don't even know that I'm doing it. And like, when I do it, when my hand hits the wall, that's like the first time I think about it. Maybe there's another me inside the one everybody sees ordering me to do things. I suppose that'd be all right, except it would be nice to know that this other person, the one inside me, was ordering me to do good things too, not only bad things."

Then Eddie Harrington paused, as though he had actually caught sight of that other person inside himself.

"I think my problems are due to my parents, 'specially my father, although I hate to blame him. Maybe I'm even a little afraid to blame him. But like, when a kid like me grows up, he kind of expects his dad and mother to be certain ways. Like, first off, he expects them to be married or not married, right? Or like with my folks, if they don't have enough money to get a divorce, let them be separate with the kids sort of knowing, over here's where your mother lives and over there's where your father lives. But none of this maybe they are together and maybe they aren't because nobody can tell because one time he's here and then he's not for a couple of days—or maybe weeks—and then he's back again. I mean, they got to make up their minds where they stand, 'specially if they got a family, kids and all.

"So the next thing I think kids got a right to expect is that their father or mother got a job. In my case I think it should be my father who has a job 'cause he ain't separated from us. They don't have a divorce, so why shouldn't he have a job? Nobody ever asks him to do anything around the house, so why shouldn't a kid like me and my sisters expect him to be working? Like with us, we never get the real picture of what's going on with my father. Not that it has to be our business, because if the guy doesn't want to tell us what's going on in his life, he don't have to. But when he isn't working, when you see him hanging around the house doing nothing—and I mean day after day, all the time—then he ought to explain it. 'Specially to me. I'm his son. And *he's* supposed to be training *me* for when

I'm a man. I got to get a job some day. But he doesn't trust us enough to tell us anything I guess, 'cause he should be telling us what's going on.

"I don't see that much of my father. Lots of guys I know, they see their father all the time, and some of 'em, they never see 'em. But not only don't I know what he does, I don't even know where he goes. If I was little, you know, like a baby just walking or talking, I wouldn't care all that much. Like, I would know how a father is supposed to be. Hell, I wouldn't even know there *is* such a thing as a father. But now, I understand all of it. He's as good as any other guy like him. I mean, he don't have any real education, any skill for doing much. He can't just join a union. They don't take anybody. A guy has to prove he can sweat pipes or fix gutters, you know, before they can even figure out what union he's supposed to join. But like with my father, he can't do that much. He wants to, he wants to work, I know that 'cause he's told us lots of times. But where's he going to get a job? Where's he going to find anything for any amount of money? He'd take anything, man. I know he would. He doesn't talk that way to us. He couldn't. I couldn't either if I was him. But he'd take anything. A guy comes to the house tomorrow and says, 'Hey, Mr. Harrington, we got a job for you shoveling shit off the dock into the river,' he'd take it in a minute. He'd ask them, 'How much the job pay?' 'specially if one of us was standing around listening to him. Maybe he'd say, 'Well let me think about it. I don't know that a guy like me wants to shovel shit for the rest of his life.' But hell, they offer him steady work for two days a week, he'd grab it.

"My father's ashamed he's out of work. You can see it just the way he's, like, afraid to look at us. He don't even want to be seen. He's hiding from us. I'd be that way too. Like, when I don't do my work in school I hide from everybody, 'specially my teachers. I don't know what they'd say but I don't want to know. My dad hides the same way. He's like a little boy. He tells me all the time, 'You got to be a man. Don't let people beat you or get the best of you, you know what I mean.' But he can't be that way himself. And you know why? 'Cause he's begging. He's a street beggar. That's all. He's begging for anything he can get and he don't like it. You know when you go 'round and see those run-down old guys begging in the street? I used to see them walking with my dad sometimes. He'd tell me, 'Never want to give people like that money. They had the strength they'd go out and find a job like the rest of us.' But now he's just like them, only he's got too much pride to go out there and be like them. Jesus, I just thought how that would feel, walking down the street with your friends and seeing all these beggars, all of them reaching out their hands like they'd take the money out of your pocket if you don't give it to them, and suddenly, there's your father, you know, begging for money that maybe he gave you that morning. I don't even know if I'd say hello to him. Fact I know I wouldn't. I'd be too embarrassed, just like my dad is now.

"I understand the way he is. I'd tell him if he gave us the chance. He shouldn't be ashamed. All of us know what's going on with jobs. He ain't the first guy out of work around here, and he sure won't be the last. It's going to get worse. I just wish he'd give us the chance to talk about it with him so he wouldn't have to keep going away all the time like he does, and I wouldn't have this other person in me telling me I got to do things that get me in trouble. Hell, I'm bound to end up in jail. Maybe meet my old man in there one of these days. The rate we're both heading there's a good chance of that too."

The lighting of fires lasted for several months. They stopped abruptly when Eddie Harrington was picked up by a policeman as he was about to ignite a pile of newspapers and garbage behind a bakery shop. The policeman had been watching as Eddie made his preparations. Believing that Eddie was going to rob the bakery when people rushed out to see the fire, the policeman chose to wait. In fact he saw Eddie merely standing nearby. Calling him a sick pyro, the policeman took him to the precinct station where, as Eddie describes it, six or seven officers questioned him.

"You should have seen them, they couldn't wait to get their hands on me. They acted like I was the number one most wanted crook in the country. I couldn't believe it. All these guys, I almost asked them how come they didn't have anything better to do with themselves than ask me all these stupid questions. I didn't say that, of course, 'cause mostly I was scared. Just the way they got the place set up makes it scary, and not just for kids. Like, the only things they have on the walls are posters of prisoners and crooks. Honest to God. You'd think they'd put something on the walls, make it a little nicer for them. They do that much at school, and there can't be no rooms in the world uglier than what we got in school. I mean they're terrible. And these cops, they got to *work* there all day and all night. You'd think they'd like it nicer.

"First they didn't do nothing with me. Just let me sit there. They put me in this room in the back somewhere, dragging me through the halls like they'd just arrested Al Capone or somebody. You could tell they weren't too excited bv it, acting tough and laughing a lot. This guy who arrested me, he laughed all the time they were taking me to the station. Then we get there and they put me in this room and nobody says nothing. I sat there and sat there and nobody ever came in, not even by accident. I could have gone outside but I just sat there. So finally this guy comes in, a cop, and he says, 'Who the hell are you? Aren't you a little young to be sitting there like that? What the hell you do anyway, rob a nursery?' And he laughs too. So I say to him, real polite, 'Can I go?' So he says, 'How the hell should I know? I don't even know why you're here so how should I know if you can go. Who booked you?' That's what he asked me. Who booked you? Like, I wanted to say to the guy, 'What do you think I did, tell the cop who picked me up that before he arrested me he had to tell me his name?' I didn't say nothing, and this guy goes away too. So I sit there another two hours and nobody comes in. I remember it started out light outside but I could see through the window it was getting darker and darker, and I was getting hungrier and hungrier.

"So finally I go out and I'm walking through the halls of the station, honest to God. I'm free as a bird walking around looking in all these rooms. And all these cops there, they saw me, none of 'em said a thing to me. I'm walking around the halls and they're going about their business. So I ask this one guy, 'Are you supposed to question me?' He goes, 'Who are you?' So I tell my name, and he yells out, 'We got an Eddie Harrington here for some reason?' and this other cop at the desk who looked like he was drunk or something, he says, 'Nope, nobody here by that name.' So the cop says I should go back to the room where I was. I could have walked out of there any time. I didn't have to talk to any of them. I could have just walked out. I could have pretended I was one of the policeman's sons, just walking around looking for my father. Then I thought, what if I walked into some room and I really did see my father, being a prisoner, although as far as I know my dad never got into trouble with cops. I think my sister and me were the first in the family.

"Anyway, I go back in this room and wait. Then, like at nine or ten o'clock—I never did know what time it was in there—this big fat cop comes in, guy with the reddest face I ever saw with all these pimples and sores all over his nose and cheeks. He comes in there and he says, 'Okay let's have it.' So I start to tell him about the fire and he stops me. He says, 'First off, who's your father?' So I tell him. Then he says, 'What's your father do?' So I tell him, 'I don't know,' 'cause I don't, and he says I'm being fresh. So I tell him again my dad don't work. So he says, 'What is he, a crook or just out of work?' So I tell him he's out of work, like for a lot of months. So the cop says, 'Call him on the phone,' and he gives me a dime. So I tell him I don't know where he is. He'd been around the house but I was afraid to tell him what happened. Then I thought, if my father gives me shit for getting into trouble starting fires, I'll tell him *he's* the reason I do it 'cause he's never around the house even when he isn't working.

"So the cop says, 'Call your home.' And I'm sitting there thinking, how come you don't fix all those pimples you got hiding your nose. So I call home with his dime 'cause, like, I did have some money with me when they arrested me but they took everything when they brought me in there. My sister Elaine, she was the only one home. She said my father wasn't around but she had a number where maybe I could get him. So I have to ask this cop with the nose for another dime. So he says, 'What the hell you think this is, a goddam bank?' He wasn't all that bad, but he was starting to think I was going to call every number in this city on his bread. Anyway, I call this number Elaine give me and this woman answers. So she says, "Yeah, he's here, who are *you?*" So I say, 'Who the hell are *you?*' *That's* when I found out about my old man, and why he goes away, and *where* he goes too, 'cause she put her hand over the phone, you know, thinking I couldn't hear but I heard everything. She goes, 'Hey, Harrington, put your pecker in your pants one minute. There's a kid on the phone says he's your son.' Then I heard him say, 'How the hell he find me here for Chrissakes? Tell him I'm not here.' She must have shaked her head 'cause he went, 'Do like I say. Just tell him I'm not here. Tell him you never heard of me.' So she gets back on the phone and does like he says. 'He never heard of anyone named Harrington, this guy here. You got the wrong number. I thought you asked for somebody else.' So I don't say nothing. Like, I was so surprised I didn't know what the hell to tell her when she said that. All this time the nose is looking at me, like he's thinking, 'What the hell is going on over there? Who the hell you talking to anyway?' So finally I tell her, and I'm starting to cry now, man. I could feel myself crying all over the goddam phone, 'Tell my father I never want to see him again. Tell him he's chicken shit.' The cop thought I was kidding. He thought I was stalling for time, and the woman hung up in my face. Bam! Like that.

"But this cop with the nose, he was all right. He made me talk to him about my father. At first I didn't want to, but then I thought, why not, I ain't got anybody else here. I was sort of interested to know what I *would* say. What I said was that I was ashamed of him and he was ashamed of himself too 'cause he didn't have a job and he didn't have anyplace to go where people respected him, which I suppose was a lot like me too. He couldn't look at my mother so he found this other woman, Elaine knows her name. I knew it but I always want to forget it. He couldn't be a man with any of us. Like, he couldn't be a husband 'cause he didn't have any respect from my mother, 'cause she only respects men with lots of money. She's told me that herself. She said all the time I was growing up, 'I'll love you. I'll always love you. I'll always do that 'cause you're my own blood. But just 'cause I'm your mother don't mean I have to respect you. You got to earn that.' So when I'd ask her what do I have to do before I earn it—not that I could care one way or the other whether my old lady respected me because I don't think she's done so much in her life that I'd respect *her* for—she'd say,

'I'll probably never respect you. You ain't going to end up too much better than your father, and there isn't a soul anywhere who's going to respect *him*.'

"You see how this not working hit all of us. He didn't like himself 'cause he couldn't be a man with her. She told him after he'd been in and out of about, Jesus, seemed like a million jobs, until he got a steady job she wouldn't sleep in the same room with him. So he told her that wasn't fair. So she goes, 'You don't think it's fair? What about the rest of us with nothing to eat and no money for clothes and living in this lousy stinking place. Kids are always screaming for something *I* can't give them because *you* ain't got any job.' We heard 'em fighting all the time, but a lot of it was a lie because we never asked for nothing when he wasn't working. We knew what was going on. Even my little sister, every time she'd open up her mouth to ask for something, one of us would smack her or drag her out of the room. My parents saw what we were doing. We were only doing it to protect *them,* but my mother lied. She told him we were always asking for things.

"So there was my old man with no job and no wife. I guess he didn't have the courage to talk about his problems to the rest of us, which I don't blame him for, 'cause if I were in his shoes I wouldn't go blabbing off to my kids about what a failure I am. I mean, it'd be hard enough just looking in the mirror every day and seeing myself. That's the thing, I'm like that too. When I'm in trouble, or think I am, I start running away. Either I really do run away or my mind's working like I was running away. So my father finds this chick who likes him even though he's old and don't have a job. Maybe he never even told her he was married or did have a job or didn't have a job. I wouldn't blame him for nothing he did after the way my mother treated him. If you ask me, she should have stood by him, done everything he told her to do. She said she wanted to be with people she could respect, which is rich men. That's what she meant. She wanted a rich guy, which is a laugh. There ain't no trick to having respect for a guy with lots of bread. What the hell's so tricky about that? 'Course you like a guy who gives you everything you want. I would too. You know what I told her? I said she'd respect a rich guy but she wouldn't love him 'cause she'd be too busy taking things he gave her to love him. She'd say she loved him, but she wouldn't. If she had any guts she would have said to my father, 'Don't go running around when you don't have a job. Stay here, we'll take care of things. We'll think of something.' But no, she had to say, 'You got no job, then you ain't going to have no wife.' So how can I hate the guy when I'm feeling sorry for him half the time and wondering whether he's alive or dead the rest of the time. I told him to go to hell that time on the phone when I found him in bed with that woman, and I don't even know if I hated him then. The worst he is is a creep, and nobody really hates a creep. They're just small little guys, little ants. Most of the time you're stepping on 'em, killing 'em, and you don't even know they're there."

Eddie Harrington was detained in the precinct station eight and a half hours at the time of his first arrest. In the end, there was no formal investigation or charge, merely a severe warning that if there were a next time, the police would, as they said, come down hard on him, even though he was only fourteen years old. If the police had learned anything from the little bit of conversation with him, it was that he was an intelligent boy who knew the law and the penalties for breaking it. They had learned too that Eddie possessed an exceptional understanding of his parents' condition. They told him that this understanding should help him to be more compassionate with his parents, not cause them hardship by getting himself in trouble. It was a typical speech, Eddie reported, the sort of "Cop Sermon" every boy in the neighborhood had heard at one time or another. Yet in this case, there was something slightly out of the ordinary. On his way out of the precinct station that evening, as he waited for a policeman to drive him home, Eddie Harrington overheard a policeman say:

"That Harrington kid? You talk to him? Kid's sharp as a buck. Smartest kid Davies ever brought in here. But sick in the mind. I'll predict right now that boy will be in here one day with a murder charge wrapped around his neck. You hear him in there?"

Eddie claims he smiled when he heard this report on himself, but it terrified him too because he had been thinking a great deal of killing someone. There was no one in particular he wished to kill; it was only an urge that never subsided. Almost every day he would fantasize murder. He might be sitting on the trolley car coming home from school and he would see an elderly gentleman sitting across from him looking old, tired, depressed. He would imagine what the man's life was like and try to put himself in the man's body so that he could feel the heaviness and sadness he observed. At first he would feel sorry for the man and wish that he could help him, if indeed the man needed help. Then he would imagine having a conversation with the man, and a whole scene would unfold.

They would be traveling somewhere on the trolley. It would be night and only a few people would be riding in the car. Eddie would strike up a conversation, letting the man see his good-natured side.

"What do you say, Dad, how's it going with you?"

"Not bad, Son," the man would answer, obviously eager to talk with Eddie.

"But you look so glum, so down in the mouth. What you need is a good, stiff drink, or a night with a broad. Which is it?"

"Nah, that's not it," the man would protest with a grin, looking a bit sheepish. "Can't get a job, that's all."

"Is *that* all it is?" Eddie would ask, letting the man hear his most casual manner. "Hell, we can always find you a job."

"There ain't no jobs, Son. I've tried. Been trying for years to get one. Shoveling shit off the dock even, if they offered it to me. Got children to feed and a wife that still can stomach the sight of me. Got to find something, or I don't know what."

"Or what, Dad?" Eddie would get serious at this point and lean across the aisle to listen more closely.

"Or else, I'm going to have to leave the world, I guess. Ain't going to live this way no more. Can't take it. Family can't take it. Times are tough and all that, but that don't help me none. What happens to the next guy ain't none of my affair. It's only what happens to *me* that matters. I get a job I'm happy, or, I can make it for a while. Wouldn't say I'm happy exactly. Without a job, though, hell, I'll cut out of here."

They were the words his own father had spoken to him.

In his fantasy, Eddie would look shocked. "You'd kill yourself just 'cause you couldn't find a job?"

By this point both Eddie and the man would be glancing down the length of the car making certain no one was listening to them.

"Kill myself tonight if I knew no job was coming. Ain't worth going on for. Not enough to be alive. They say, long as you got your health you got it all, that's a crock, young man, a crock in the alley! You can make it knowing you're dying of some disease if you got something to do with yourself. It ain't the thought of dying that kills you, it's the thought that there ain't no sane reason in the world to get out of bed in the morning if you ain't got no job and you ain't got a person in the world who could give a running shit for you because you ain't got one. I know. I've been there more than once, more than twice; fact is, all the time now."

"And you're ready to die? Like now? Tonight?" At this point in the fantasy Eddie Harrington always did the same thing. Upon expressing his incredulity at the man's eagerness to die, he would try to compute his father's age, but he never could reach a figure that satisfied him. No matter how he reasoned, he invariably ended up making his father too old. Then he would determine to ask his father the next time he spoke with him, but he never did. He thought about the question when speaking with his father, but he never dared ask him directly.

"Listen, old man," he would say as his fantasy resumed, "I'm going to do you a favor, a favor of a lifetime."

The man would respond with almost childlike curiosity. "What you got?" And as he would lean forward awaiting Eddie's proposition, Eddie could actually see him becoming youthful, content. His face would be transformed and his posture would change.

"I'm going to take that death problem away from you."

Still the eagerness and anticipation would gleam on the elderly man's face. He would look up at Eddie, as if the boy were twice his height. "But how?"

Then, as his hands began to perspire, his breathing quickened, his nostrils widened, Eddie Harrington would imagine himself becoming crazed with a sadistic passion. He would see himself standing up in front of the elderly man and producing a large, link-steel chain. He would yell at the few passengers in the car to get off and they would run away whimpering and screaming, covering up their faces for fear that Eddie would remember them and come looking for them. Then Eddie would begin to destroy the man. Starting with the man's legs, he would beat him with the chain, being careful that it would not whip around and smash him at the same time. With all his might he would swing the chain at the man's chest and hear the ribs crack and the man cry out in pain. Then he would use every muscle in his body to sling the chain so that it would not only crash against the man's skull, but wrap around it several times, splitting open the cheeks and the bones around the eyes and ears. Blood would pour out onto the seats and the floor of the car. The man would be soaked in blood, his face splintered and contorted in the ugliest way. And Eddie Harrington's heart would beat faster and faster until he could practically feel the pressure of his blood rising to the point of exploding. He would imagine that he was laughing and crying, swearing, yelling, and whispering all at once. He would feel gratified and fulfilled, guilty and ashamed. And always the man's broken body would fall over frontward, thumping upon the dirty rubber matted floor of the trolley car and landing against Eddie's own legs in a sickening hulk. Eddie would kick himself free and want to vomit or urinate on the man. He would say aloud:

"There you are old man. Lucky you aren't my real father. Now you don't have nothing to be sad about no more. Now you don't have to get up every morning wondering, do I have a job today or don't I? Will my wife and kids like me because I do have a job or I don't have a job? Now I don't have to look nobody in the face again and let 'em see what sort of a bum I really am. Rich man or beggar, they'll never know when they find me crushed to death. If I died for natural causes everybody would say he just quit 'cause he couldn't get work, chicken-shit son of a bitch. He could have found something if he really hunted for it. He found a chick didn't he, and he wasn't that young, you know, and he didn't have no money. Didn't even have a job, so how could he have money? Nobody's going to say that, or, 'I feel so sorry for his wife and his kids, 'specially that little boy of his. Ain't got no husband or father, now only because the man was a failure and a quitter, just like his wife always said he was.' No sir, they're going to find your body, my friend, all mangled up, and nobody's going to want to know whether you were a success or a failure, a good man or a bad man. All they're going to do is vomit when they see the kind of shape you're in and feel sorry for you. Fact is, they'll feel so sorry for you, they won't even bother to find out who you were. They might never know you're as poor as you are. Hell, they might even take you as being one of those rich guys, shelling out money to everybody that my mother says she has so much respect for. So long, old man."

Eddie Harrington did not stop at setting fires in the safe confines of children's sandboxes. He didn't even stop at setting fires in places where serious conflagrations might have resulted. Once he was so frightened by a fire he started in a school yard several miles from his house—he had made a special trip to get there—that he telephoned the fire department. When they arrived Eddie concocted a detailed description of two boys who started the fire. The police were impressed by his description and asked his name, address, and telephone number. He gave them a false name and address and the telephone number of the woman his father visited. He never found out whether the police called her, but it would have made little difference to anyone if they had. She would say she never heard of Eddie Harrington or Bill Trent, the name he had contrived. It always impressed him that on the spur of the moment, and not without pressure, he had invented such a reasonable sounding name as Bill Trent. I'm going to be one helluva criminal, he thought, riding the trolley home after the fire at the Halliday School had been extinguished. There was, however, a real William Trent, someone Eddie Harrington knew about.

Eddie Harrington, Senior's, last so-called steady job had been with the Amos Coal Company. He had told his wife the job looked secure. Money was tight in the coal industry and there would be layoffs coming, but the senior Harrington was not especially worried since he was high in the seniority ladder of the men in his department.

There were eight of them, and he was second in line behind the foreman. The entire department would be closed before the company laid off Ed Harrington. Besides, he had been a well-liked employee. Even Frank Amano said that Ed Harrington deserved to stay with Amos more than any other man, and everybody knew that Frank Amano never complimented anyone, especially someone with whom he was competing for a job. They told a story about Frankie Amano losing his job in a car plant in Michigan. When the news came he made inquiries and learned the names of the men who would be retained. When he discovered that three men he worked with were scheduled to be kept on, he broke the arm of one of them, threatened to kill him if he ever told what happened, and arranged to get reinstated in the company as a substitute. The men who despised Frank Amano said he was so ruthless he'd kill his own children if it meant his getting a job. The men who were terrified of Frank Amano said people get ruthless when they're out of work. It meant a lot to Ed Harrington when Frank Amano told him that he personally would make certain that Amos Coal would close its doors for good before they fired him.

Young Eddie was with his father the day the two men talked. He remembered Frank Amano as a tall, dark man with pitch-black eyes and the hairiest arms he had ever seen. He was afraid that Mr. Amano wanted to fight his father and relieved when it turned out they were friends.

"You like that guy?" Eddie Harrington asked his son after Frank Amano had driven off in a brand new Chevrolet. "Huh? What'd you think of him?"

Little Eddie didn't know what to say. Secretly he admired the dark, hairy man, although he was also afraid of him. But he sensed his father's attitude and shrugged his shoulders. "I don't know. What do *you* think?"

"I'll tell you exactly," Ed Harrington told his son. "I love Frank Amano for one reason: I always know where I am with him. That's a great thing to know with another guy, just exactly where you are with him. When he says he's pulling for me and that this company will shut down before I lose my job, I know he knows the place is in real trouble and he'd do everything in his power to keep me out of any job in this city if it looks to him like I'm standing in his way."

"That's what I thought," little Eddie answered, hiding his confusion, but not his admiration for his father.

"No it ain't," his father said suddenly. "You were taken in by him the same way I was. You believed every word he said. But you'll see what happens when he talks to Trent. Bill Trent got to be foreman 'cause he'd do anything anybody tells him. He's as big a liar as Amano is, only he don't have none of Amano's guts. Bill Trent's a phony. He's worse than Frank Amano because everybody walks over him. Even a kid your size could scare the piss out of him."

This was the conversation young Eddie Harrington remembered when the police asked for his name. Bill Trent, he had answered, for an instant unable to place the name. Then it all came back to him. The walk with his father, his misjudgment of Frank Amano, his father's bitterness toward Bill Trent, and of course the end of the story, which was Bill Trent firing his father for reasons that were never explained. And then there was his father's parting lunch with Frank Amano and Bill Trent, and the two of them expressing their unhappiness and surprise, and promising to help Ed Harrington find another job.

Eddie Harrington remembers his father coming home that afternoon after the lunch and telling his mother how he was going into their savings to buy a gun. "What the hell do I have to lose anymore?" his son heard him bellowing. "Might as well get a little bit of goddam satisfaction out of my life. Ain't had a fuckin' shred of it in forty years. I'd only be doing everybody coming up behind me a favor if I got rid of that son of a bitch Amano. Trent will choke in his own shit. Is anybody home?"

"Eddie," his mother had answered sharply.

The answer did not stop Ed Harrington. He went on railing against the men who had betrayed him.

"Miserable bastards," he had screamed. "You work your goddam ass off for years, for *years* goddamit, and what the hell does it bring you. They screw you behind your back, in front of your eyes. What the hell they give a goddam about? They care if you work? Dog eat dog out there? My ass. It's man eat man and those bastards always win. They'll win when I'm dead and buried too. They got two kinds of people in this world. They got suckers like me and they got the people who suck. Amano, Trent, all those bastards, they suck. They find people like me and they high-mouth us, every one of us. 'Oh, you'll get the job, Harrington. You'll be the first to stay, last to leave. You been here the longest, we'll give 'em all kinds of shit if they mess with you, Harrington, you little Irish asshole. We're rooting for you, Harrington. Standing up there next to you, behind you, in front of you, anywhere you want us to be 'cause you're our guy, Harrington. You aren't alone in the world, Harrington. You got a family to feed. Nice wife, nice daughters, good-looking son. You got it made, Eddie baby, ain't no one going to touch you without coming through us first!'

"Miserable cock suckers. Chrissakes, that son of a bitch Amano was bullshitting me right in front of my kid. Right the fuck in front of my goddam *kid*. I asked him, two weeks ago, less than that, I asked him, 'Eddie, what'd you think of Frank Amano? What do you think of the man?' And the kid's taken in. He's ready to tell me he thinks Amano is God's fucking gift to the goddam human race. Frank Amano, baby, I know your kind. I can smell you out ten blocks away, a half a fuckin' country away. You're in Detroit and you hear something's happening in Pittsburgh, you go, man. You eat people and you spit 'em out to take care of yourself. You want to know about Frank Amano and Bill Trent, who by the way is the biggest bullshitter 'cause his name is Grady, or O'Grady, and he's afraid some folks will steal his little goddam job from him if they find out he's a mick? So he passes. One day he's a little Irish Catholic, then you see him two days later and maybe he's a Presby or a Methodist, or whatever the hell he needs. Christ, he'd pass as a goddam Jew or nigger in blackface if he could save his job or take someone else's from him.

"You want to tell me times are tight, okay, times are tight. They've never been this bad. It's hitting everybody. Okay, so I'm just part of the great old American system. Okay, so now I know, so what the hell good's it going to do me? I got kids I got to feed. And what the hell is anybody, my family, anybody supposed to think when all they hear about is me losing my fucking job all the time? What the hell you supposed to say to them? 'Hey, Daddy, how come you ain't working and Frank Amano and Bill Trent are? Huh? How come that is? We see their kids, we play with 'em all the time. How come you're always home and their fathers are always working?' What do I say? They got someone going to give me a little advice about all that? Sure, they got things to tell you to say. You just say, 'Well, Son, I'll tell you what the story is. Come sit here on Daddy's lap and he'll tell you the facts of life. You see, Son, guys like Frank Amano and Bill Trent can be explained real simple. Say there was one job in the world left for a man to do and two people who might take the job. They're one of the guys, see, and the guy competing for the job is their own son. Now mind you, their son is just a newborn baby still in the hospital, two days old. They still got him there in one of those cribs 'til he's old enough to get out of the hospital. Just like they had you in when you were born. Frank Amano and Bill Trent would go into that nursery in that hospital, and thinking their boss just might go crazy and give the one job in the world to this little two-day-old kid lying there in his own piss and shit, they go in there and squeeze the little kid to death so they can make sure they got the job. Then they go right out, have a drink, and bring their goddam wife a bunch of flowers and a big card that says, 'Jesus Christ, Hon, you know how bad I feel. I wanted that little fellow in there just as bad as you did. I can't imagine what kind of animal could have done that to him.' "

Eddie Harrington, who had been curled up on his bed, the heels of his hands pressed against his ears in a futile effort to keep from listening, heard his mother cry out to his father:

"Jesus Christ, Ed, you're mad. You're really sick. They've made you sick, or the job thing has, or something has, and I don't give a damn what it is. But you are *sick*. And I forbid you to be near the kids when you're like this. You better get out of here. Jesus, you're mad. Killing a two-day-old baby. What the hell are you talking about? There's two kinds of people in the world all right, sick ones and healthy ones, and brother, I don't know much, but you sure as hell aren't one of the healthy ones. You're out of your mind. Killing babies? What the hell's with you? Get out. Get out!"

Young Eddie heard a chair fall over and a noise that sounded like someone being hit with a cushion. He was too terrified to open the door and see what his parents were doing, much less let himself imagine what they looked like in their fury. Suddenly, the door to his room flew open and his father was standing there. Ed Harrington looked surprised to find his son huddled on the bed, but not embarrassed.

"You hear?" he asked in a calm voice.

His son merely nodded.

"Good. Might be the best education about life you'll ever get. You hear the part about choking little babies?"

Eddie Harrington could not move. He could neither nod nor speak. His mouth was dry and the palms of his hands were covered with perspiration.

"You heard," his father said. "I'll tell you something else just to make certain you got it in your head for good." All the while he held the doorknob in one hand and the door frame in the other, his large fingers gripping tightly to the wood until the tips of his fingernails showed white crescents. "There's only one thing in life that matters, and that's working, working steady at whatever the hell you do. It ain't important whether you choose it or find it or stumble on it. All I know is you got to work, regular. Every day. Monday, Tuesday, Wednesday, Thursday, Friday. Saturday and Sunday too if you need the money. But you shouldn't have to if you put in an honest forty hours. And you fight for every job and fight to keep it as if they were trying to take away your two arms. You get it? Your two arms. Don't believe nobody. Listen to nobody. The only thing that talks is the job. When you got it you got everything. When you lose it, or when those bastards out there take it away from you, you got nothing. They can throw every word in the goddam dictionary at you and you still don't have nothing. You got that?"

Still his son did not move.

"Get a job, then get yourself a gun. A big one. Keep it with you loaded so the first guy that starts messing with you gets it right between the old eyes. Let 'em take your wife, your home, your car, anything they like, but die before they take your job away. 'Cause you're going to be like me, 'cause you're my blood. And you're going to die the same way I do. With a job you got life; without it, you're long since dead. You get what I'm saying?"

Eddie nodded.

"I'll be back. Look after your mother." Ed Harrington, Senior, closed the door. His son heard the door to the outside open and close and his father slowly descending the concrete steps.

Ed Harrington's speech to his son had been perfectly direct, and delivered with calmness and strength. He knew exactly what he had wanted to say, almost as if he had been waiting for just that moment to say it. Yet, it was almost impossible to believe that he could have been as calm and straightforward when, throughout the talk, such heavy tears had flowed from his eyes. He must have known he was crying, but he didn't let that stop him. Perhaps this was because his son too had been crying, and there was no use for either man to speak about it.

At fifteen, not long after his birthday, Eddie Harrington was arrested by the police for stealing money from a grocery store. When taken to the police station he was also charged with setting fires on six different occasions. One of the fires he allegedly set had destroyed an old wooden building near the railroad tracks that had long been condemned and therefore vacated. As it happened, a little boy was playing in the building and perished in the fire. This meant that Eddie was also charged with involuntary manslaughter. He stayed in jail thirteen months awaiting trial. When at last his case was taken to court, the judge ruled that there was insufficient evidence to prove his role in the setting of four fires, but ample evidence to find him guilty of arson in the other two, as well as the robbery. He was sentenced to prison for a term to run no less than one year, no more than three years.

At the sentencing, the judge apologized to Eddie Harrington and his mother for the way the boy had been detained. Mrs. Harrington nodded as though accepting the judge's words. Eddie merely stood still, looking tough but beaten. When the judge asked Eddie whether his father was in the courtroom, Eddie answered quietly, "No." When the judge then asked, "Is your father alive?" the boy thought for a conspicuously long time. His mother too remained silent. Finally he looked down and mumbled, "I don't know. If he is, he wouldn't be here. He'd be out someplace looking for a job!"

6

We Bad Little People in Here,
We Get to Eat

Angela Wittenberg is known to her friends as the Bat Lady, because in the winter she wears a long, dark cape with two large black buttons at the collar. Fifteen years old, Angela is a small girl, barely five feet high, with long, black hair and deep-set brown eyes. When she walks, her cape drags on the ground, giving her the appearance of a moving mountain. Angela's aunt, Margaret Wittenberg, says the cape was a present to Angela from a man whose name she cannot remember. Angela claims she stole the cape from a department store. Her younger sister, Patty, says the cape was a gift from Harry the Barber, who liked the way Angela stood up to the judge the first time she was taken to court, three years ago, when she was twelve. Apparently, when the judge asked her to name the young people with whom she had broken into a foodmart, Angela replied loudly, "If you can't find them don't expect me to give you their names."

On that occasion the judge let her go. He told her that she was headed for no good. It was a bad sign being brought into his court at such a young age, and besides, he knew the police record of her older brother Arnold. "What Arnold did ain't got nothing to do with me," she told the judge. "No one in my family talks with him no more." She told the judge the same thing when she appeared before him less than a year later. Again he spoke about Arnold who was then serving time in one of the state institutions that went by the name of an industrial school. Each time she went to court, Harry Barboza, the young man everyone called Harry the Barber because he always carried a barber's shears and a cuticle scissors in his car, went with her. Angela said Harry was her moral support. Arnold said Harry was there to make certain she didn't mention his name to the judge or any of the lawyers. Patty didn't know for certain why Harry hung around the courtroom. She assumed that he was one of Angela's boyfriends. With bitterness, she described Angela as a "loose kid who'd turn a trick for a nickel if that was all she could get."

Soon after her fifteenth birthday, Angela Wittenberg was arrested for breaking and entering. It was her third appearance before the same judge in the same courtroom, the fourth time, by her own admission, that she had broken into the same food store. Unlike the other times, on this occasion she stole money that had been left in one of the registers, as well as two shopping bags of food. Calling her hopeless and blaming her, her parents, and society too, the judge sentenced her to a term of no less than one year in a state correctional institution for girls. Angela told him she was glad to go, at least she'd be warm during the winter. When the judge said he never wanted to see her back in his court or any court again, Angela grinned and said, "I'd never make a promise I can't keep. I'll be back. If you aren't here I'll just have to see someone else then, right?" The judge turned away from her. Someone in the rear of the courtroom clapped.

The prospect of spending a year with girls her own age at the correctional institution didn't seem that bad to Angela. Shelly Kane, a seventeen-year-old girl who had served a year and a half at the institution, described the place as the best poor man's boarding school around. Shelly was a former girl friend of Arnie's and one of the few friends of her brother Angela cared for. If Shelly said jail was all right, then it was all right. But it was seven months into her sentence before Angela was actually taken to the correctional institution. During this time, owing either to a mistake in the records office or, as she said, because there were people in the court who were out to get her, she was placed in a county jail for women. Until one week before she left the jail, she was the youngest woman there. Just before she left for the correctional institution to which the judge had remanded her, a fourteen-year-old girl who had been charged with prostitution was assigned to the adjoining cell. At first Angela was grateful to have someone her own age as a friend, but by the second day the two girls were fighting in the yard and had to be separated. Finally Angela was transferred to the correctional institution to which she was remanded seven months previously.

My own visits with Angela in jail began at this time, although I had known her and her family for several years before she had gotten into trouble with the law. It took little prodding to get her to speak about her experiences of being incarcerated in a county institution for women.

"Lots of the women there," she told me, "were real decent to me. Some of 'em even liked me. They pretended like I was one of their own kids. So they'd make things for me or give me the presents people had brought to them. They didn't lie about it. They'd tell me someone brought in some food, like, to them, but they wanted me to have it. Or maybe they'd give me cigarettes or clothes. I didn't ever have no clothes I ever liked. Me and my sisters always looked the worst in school. My mother never thought it was important to have her kids looking nice. She was an ugly old bitch and she knew it. So she probably figured since I ain't no winner I ain't about to make my own kids look any good. We never had no money, but there was enough one way or another that we could have looked a lot better than we did. I remember once my mother got this hundred-dollar bill. Some guy gave it to her. She showed it to us. We were dancing around, making up all these ideas about things we would buy, you know. So what does she do? She goes out and buys a couple of little things for herself, nothing really great, then she spends the rest of the money buying presents for all these crummy friends of hers. She didn't buy nothing for us. Nothing.

"So when these women in there gave me presents, you better believe I took them. I knew I shouldn't, but I told myself, maybe this is what I got coming from that hundred-dollar bill she got from that guy. I knew what these women wanted. Guard told me the first night to look out for some of them, but I didn't care. I mean, you get what you get, whatever's coming to you. So like this first night a bunch of us are sitting around doing something, I don't remember what, and this one woman, Pokey they called her—good looking, maybe forty, something like that—she comes up behind me and pulls up my hair you know, and gives me this big wet kiss on the back of my neck. Everybody saw her do it. They saw her coming at me too but none of 'em said nothing, like to warn me or something, you know? So I swung around and rapped her right up alongside her head.

Right? So she falls on top of me on this easy chair I was sitting on and we're going at it, hitting and pulling each other's hair, and all of a sudden I feel someone feeling me up. Right in the middle of this fight I look down and see this other freak, this Irene what's her name, touching me down there and kissing me. So I start to yell for help but none of them does nothing. They're just watching and clapping and making sure we ain't making too much noise. So then like, you got all these people wrestling and humping each other. So pretty soon I figure, what the hell, there's nothing else to do in here so I let this Irene get off on me and when she was done I let a few others do, you know, like she done. That's all. Nobody said nothing.

"Another night this other woman comes up to me in the hall with a goddam tonic bottle. You believe this? I goes, 'What the hell you think you're going to do with *that?*' She goes, 'Come on baby lady, let's see what you got under there.' So she starts to lift up my skirt and I push her away, only she laughs. Then she's coming at me again, only this time she's starting to take off her dress. No kidding. She ain't got anything on underneath. So here I am, fifteen years old, standing in this goddam corridor of this goddam jail with a sex maniac coming at me with a root beer bottle in her hand. And she ain't kidding either. I ain't about to yell for no one 'cause when they caught you messing around like that they'd put you both in solitary for four, maybe five, days. And when you've been in there like I was—they put me in there the first time 'cause they heard I was going to try to escape after a show one night, which was a lie—you know you'll do anything, including getting raped, before you'll go back.

"So I start pulling off my own dress real slowly and she starts to calm down. Like before, she looked like she could either shove that bottle up inside me or split my face open with it. But when she sees maybe I'm going to get it on with her, she kind of relaxes. So then I say, 'Take it easy, okay, 'cause I'm on the rag.' I thought that would stop her, which it did, sort of. Only she says, 'Okay, I'll leave you alone only let me suck your tits.' I figured why not, the poor woman'd probably been in there a hundred years without seeing nobody half my age. Lots of 'em have real good bodies still. I mean, they don't look like no twenty-year-old chick, but they look pretty decent, some of 'em. Even the ones who've had kids, you know. They got those little like scars on their stomachs and their tits look all strange. But hell, I was the youngest there. I was the best lay they had. I figured that's probably why they put me in there in the first place. Somebody's got to let 'em do it to 'em. Why not? They ain't got nothing in their lives to look forward to but living with all these queers and perverts and sex maniacs. I figured I'd be getting out pretty soon. No one would know, or if they did they'd understand.

"You go to jail, baby, they don't turn you off. You just keep on coming, wanting more, just like on the outside. Some of those girls could wait, but not all of 'em. When you got men, you take 'em, but if all you got is women, then that's what you take. Beggar takes whatever they give him, and like I say, lots of 'em in there were all right to me. They gave me stuff. What the hell, doin' it that way with a chick ain't all that bad. I ain't up to doin' it the rest of my life, but you get used to it. Anyway, the name of the game in there is survive. Sometimes you fight, sometimes you lie, like I tried to do with that one woman, and sometimes you just say to yourself, all right Angela, baby, settle down, lie back and just hope the guy who made that tonic bottle knew what he was doing 'cause if it breaks in there you're going to be pissing out the pieces 'til they set you in the ground and shovel in the dirt on you. So she's breathing like some wild beast and you're thinking about this factory on Western Ave where they make Coke bottles wondering whether they use high-grade glass. So what else do you want to know about my days in the *ladies* penitentiary?"

Angela and I met regularly during her stay at the correctional institution. Life here was very different from the months in the women's county jail. Most of our discussions centered around day-by-day concerns, her friendships, the plans she was making for when she got out, and her interest in people on the outside who had never come to visit her. There was no question about her sadness and her overriding feeling of hopelessness. One could easily see that, without a great deal of help, she was destined to return to this or some other comparable institution. The horrors of the women's prison were hardly a deterrent. If life went well outside, she would say, then she would do her best to stay on the outside. If life went sour, and there was nothing else to do, then she wouldn't think twice about breaking into a store for money or clothes or shoes, or perhaps just for fun. If she got caught and sentenced, and imprisoned for longer periods of time, then so be it.

"It's warm in these prisons," she would tell me, her voice flat, all emotion concealed. "No matter how cold the winter gets outside, it's always warm in here. They give you three squares a day, usually they're lousy ones, but they come. You know they're going to be there, and you know what time they're going to be there. And there they are. What else you need? They even have turkey on Christmas and Thanksgiving, and that's one helluva lot more than I ever got on the outside. I remember one Christmas when my mother walked out on all of us. Five, six days she was gone. On the day before Christmas she bought us this little tree too. I was only about eight and we were really excited, you know. We knew we wouldn't be getting nothing good for presents, but we had this tree and everybody put stuff on it. It looked all right too. So the next day she goes away, probably with some guy—I never did find out where she went—and not only did we freeze and have no presents like we knew we wouldn't have, she didn't even leave us with no food. And 'cause it was Christmas there weren't no stores open, so there we were. So you know what happened? We ended up eating steak because my brother Arnie and two of his friends threw a brick through some butcher's window miles from where we lived, you know, and brought it home. So we ate without her, the old bitch. She came back, like a week later, never said a thing to us. Didn't even ask us did we eat. So it's all right in here 'cause we eat. No matter what my mother does out there with all you good people, we bad little people in here, we get to eat."

As surprising as it seems, Angela Wittenberg claims that for the first several months of her imprisonment, she actually believed that she had been placed in the proper institution even though several of the inmates argued with the authorities that she had been improperly assigned to an adult prison. But Angela says she never understood the misassignment.

"How was I supposed to know? They grab you out of the courtroom, put you in some jail, then they take you out of there and put you someplace else. You don't know where they're going. Ain't no one in there that'll tell you what's happening to you. The only people who give a shit for you, you know, like they'll say nice things to you or try to help you in some way, they're the ones who don't know nothing at all. The pigs, these horses' asses who push you in and out of cars, they know, but they lie to everybody. They'd probably lie to their old man. So how could I know? Lots of times I said to myself, 'Hey, how come I'm so young and everybody else in here is so old?' But I figured, maybe they want to split up the kids my age who get in trouble. Most of the old ones, they ain't going to do nothing. But the young ones, maybe they got to split 'em up.

"I guess I found out about this mistake, or whatever you would call it, about four months after I got there. First, one of the inmates told me. Then this one guard who I didn't like all that much, she told me the same thing. Even when they told me it still didn't make a helluva lot of difference. Just 'cause they say you're in the wrong place don't mean they're going to move you right away. Like with me, they told me in February and I was still in there in May. I figured, they're giving me clean clothes, they're giving me food, I'm only getting raped once every couple of weeks, what I got to complain about? I never said nothing. I didn't even talk to my family about it. My sister was all bothered by it, you know, but I didn't care. 'Course when I got into the place I was supposed to be in, then I got angry 'cause there they *did* take care of us better. I had some classes once in a while and a lot more interesting things to do. I had a few friends in there. Good ones, although I liked some of those old bitches in the first place too. Some of 'em were all right. Sometimes young kids, you know, like they need older people once in a while. I suppose we make 'em feel young, and what do they got to look forward to? Like, the girls in the second place are young, most of 'em are getting out soon, so what do they care if they lose a couple, three years. You don't get it back but it ain't that big a loss.

"I wonder a lot about why they put me in the wrong place. I heard they put a lot of kids my age in these places. I figured in my case it was either a mistake or they were trying to tell me something. Like, maybe they thought if I saw what the worst place was like I'd stay out of trouble. You know, if you let the kid see the worst punishment maybe she'll stay clean. But I ain't going to stay clean. I can say I am, make all these sweet promises, but I'll be back in one of these places again, maybe with the girls in the old ladies' home, like I used to call it. Seein' all these different prisons don't make a person decide whether they're going to break the law. You can make every promise in the book, swear on your life like people do, you know, and it don't mean nothing. You take, like, one night and you get stoned and you ain't got money or any place to go, and nobody in the world's got a job for you, and maybe you got a lot of people you owe money to, you know, and you'll get into a lot of trouble if you don't pay 'em back, you better believe you'll do something like break into some place or grab somebody's purse in the street. You *got* to do it. You don't *decide* these things, you're forced to do 'em. You don't do 'em you're dead, so what's the big deal? So I'll be back, only next time, if they send me to the old ladies' home, I'm going in there with a chastity belt, 'cause I've got to be protected when those maniacs come at me.

"Maybe a lawyer could figure this out for me, but it seems like with all the smart people they got walking around someone ought to be able to figure out a better way to help kids. There's always going to be kids like me getting into trouble. Right? Seein' lousy prisons ain't going to stop nobody, like I say. Electric chair and gassing people don't stop 'em from murdering people. So you'd think they'd find a better way somehow. I lost my education in the prison. That shouldn't have been. That was maybe the only good thing I had going for me. So now I ain't got that either. So I got to do my best, walk the straight and narrow like they say, but I got the same blood my brother Arnie's got. I'll be back. Fix up the cells, ladies, the Bat Lady is for sure going to return."

7

They Got Anger Pushing 'Em in One Direction,
Fright Pushing 'Em in Another

It goes without saying that the world has known tougher
people than Johnny O'Dea, the sixteen-year-old boy whose
neighbors on Avers and Beloit Streets called "The Plague."
Everyone has stories of the toughest person they knew in
their school or block or apartment building, and everyone is
convinced that *their* nominee for the toughest is really the
toughest. That is how the people in the district they called
Garyville thought of Johnny O'Dea. One wouldn't think he
was so tough just from looking at him, but a few words with
him changed any first impressions.

The peculiar thing about the O'Dea boy, his neighbors
said, was that for a boy with such anger he actually looked

rather sweet, as though he could have been a nice boy. One could see their point. Johnny O'Dea was not large for his age. His wavy, black hair was always neatly combed, though never slick. His nose, which had been broken in a fight when he was twelve, was twisted slightly and wider actually than it was flat. His most unusual feature was his skin. He had the smoothest, clearest skin anyone had ever seen, even on a woman. It was without a mark or blemish, perfect, even when Johnny was dirty and perspiring. In fact, perspiration made his skin even more attractive, for the moisture around his eyes and across his forehead gave it a sheen, making it appear translucent. Girls who attended school with Johnny O'Dea said they would give anything for his hair and his skin, but you could keep the rest of him.

It was true that Johnny O'Dea had few friends. There were several boys who ran around with him, like Alvin Pickering, the boy they called Pick, and Stevie Wiley, whom Johnny called Stevie Wonder, but there were no truly close friends. Older boys exploited him and laughed at him behind his back. Some of the younger ones claimed they looked up to him, but even they were repelled by his toughness and constant need to fight. Some people admitted they were scared of Johnny O'Dea because he would fight anybody for any reason, and because of his notorious unpredictable quality—flying into a rage over nothing at all. One might be walking with him, having a pleasant conversation, when suddenly he would pound his fist into someone or hurl vicious insults at a person passing by.

Even the Pick had to admit he was rarely at ease with Johnny O'Dea.

"You can't never let your guard down with him," the Pick would say. "Walking with him, say, to the flicks or going somewhere to get a sandwich, you know, is like being in the ring with this quick boxer, one of these flyweight guys, you know, here one minute, gone the next. You never know where you are with a guy like him. I mean, if he likes you, it's all right, it's better than all right 'cause the guy wouldn't have no worry about taking someone on 'cause he insulted you. Don't make no difference to O'Dea who gets insulted—him, me, somebody else—he's in for the fight. Big kid, small kid, he's going in. If he gets his guts knocked out, then he gets his guts knocked out. If he wins, he wins. Only thing wrong is that sometimes you don't get the feeling he's got anybody he's going to trust. Like today, maybe, I'm walking with him and somebody says something about me that Johnny don't like. I can take it, don't bother me none, but he decides he don't like it. So boom, I don't even see it start and he's already fighting. Then two hours later, and this happens, he'll hear something I said and decide he don't like it or he won't believe something I told him, and all of a sudden I get a shot in the ribs. Just like that. No reason. He don't ask me what's going on, he just hits, and he'll say, 'Don't fuck me over, Picknick. I'll rub you out quick as that, baby. Don't fuck me over. I don't need you either.'

"Like that's maybe his favorite expression. He'll tell that to everybody. He'll say it like he don't feel nothing inside him at all: 'Don't need you either baby.' I bet I heard him say that a thousand times. Girls, boys, everybody. I heard him tell a teacher once to fuck off or something like that. Then he comes out with that saying, 'I don't need you either baby.' That woman was scared. It was all over her face, man, she was scared. Hell, *I* was scared, but she didn't do nothing. It's because the way he says it. Like, he's trying to scare you, which he does, but at the same time, you're feeling sorry for the guy, you know what I mean. It's like with one hand he's hitting you in the face and with the other hand he's sort of breaking your heart, making you feel sad for him. I can't explain it better. 'Course his background tells you a lot about him, for whatever that does. I mean, when he's beating the shit out of someone or scaring some little kid half to death in a dark alley somewhere, I don't think nobody'd be too interested in his background. But he hasn't had it all that easy."

In fact, it is difficult to determine Johnny O'Dea's background. It is known that he was put up for adoption by his mother before he was born. It is said that his father wanted the baby but his mother refused to keep it. In anger, his father said that if the baby were "orphaned" he would leave his wife. Johnny was orphaned and his father left. It is not certain therefore that his name at birth was John. Surely it was not O'Dea. One story goes that his name was William Ilman, Ilman being his mother's maiden name. Allegedly, Mrs. Ilman put her surname on the birth certificate and named the boy William after her brother, who had died in an industrial accident. This story, however, has been refuted. When the boy was two years old, he was placed in a foster home. His foster parents, Elsie and Armando Buquet, separated six months after Johnny came to live with them. Fearing that a separation would mean forfeiting her rights to the child, Elsie immediately had a man move in with her, hoping that the social service agency would never learn of the divorce.

Her deception lasted almost two years. Finally it was discovered that the man she was living with was not her husband but one William Ilman. A long, complicated round of hearings ensued and the result was that the boy was taken from her and placed in a second orphanage, not the one in which he previously had lived.

After a year and a half, a second set of foster parents was found for the boy. Indeed, Peter and Cynthia O'Dea were willing to foster as many as three children. Getting on in years and unable to have children of their own, they saw no reason not to have a large family as soon as possible. As they appeared to be a stable family and Peter's job paid a decent wage, the orphanage arranged for them to have the boy who was called Johnny and a little girl Rosie who was six months old. The O'Deas could not have been happier. Their quiet, drab home was now a veritable nursery, and they cherished the noise of children at any time of the day or night. Nothing was too good for Johnny and Rosie. The O'Deas would give up anything if it meant doing something nice for their children. Strangely, the children resembled one another. Indeed, the O'Deas decided they would raise their son and daughter to believe that they were actually brother and sister. Perhaps it would give them an additional sense of security, they reasoned.

There was much rebuilding to do with Johnny. At age five and a half he had been orphaned twice and fostered twice and was deeply upset when he had to leave the second orphanage where he liked the nuns and was beginning to get close to some of the other children, all of whom he imagined were his real brothers and sisters. Moreover, he had come to believe that Elsie Buquet was his mother. He never could decide which of the men he had known was his real father, but about Elsie he was certain. This belief caused an unusual dilemma for the O'Deas as to what they should tell the boy. He would not be swayed from the notion that Elsie was his mother, and it would make no sense to tell him that Peter O'Dea was his father. They could explain that his parents had died, but that might frighten him more than what had actually happened. Then too, someone had to be prepared to explain the disappearance of Armando Buquet, the man Johnny would logically consider to be his father.

Despite all the problems, Johnny and Rosie O'Dea were growing into lively, gentle, and happy children. They managed fine with other children, although both showed a bit of shyness in their encounters with people outside their home. But all of this was seen as normal. Johnny had periods where he ate little, a problem that troubled his new mother. He might even go two days without eating anything at all.

When his parents asked him why he wouldn't eat, he would answer, "I'm too full" or "I hate food. It makes me sick." But then, just as the O'Deas would be beside themselves with concern, Johnny would wake up complaining of hunger and ask for cereal, jelly sandwiches, cookies, and milk, and everything was fine again. And he never looked the worse for wear from his fasting. His adult teeth were coming in just at the right time, he was not underweight, and his gorgeous complexion was as beautiful as it always had been.

In the month of Johnny O'Dea's seventh birthday, Cynthia O'Dea received a telephone call from a man calling himself Teddy Grimsley. He wanted to see her right away. When she demanded to know his business, Mr. Grimsley told her that he had traced down the identity of the boy she called Johnny. "His real name," Teddy Grimsley told her in a voice that shook with emotion, "wasn't Johnny at all. It was Robert Stickles Grimsley and he's my son and I want him back!"

Cynthia O'Dea felt as though she had been shot. With her husband out of town for the day on business, she had no one to turn to for help. She asked him whether there was proof of the boy's real name. Ted Grimsley had a photostat of a birth certificate. He had carefully traced the whereabouts of his child through two orphanages and two foster homes. He could prove the boy was his own. The girl Rosie was not involved in this, he assured Cynthia. It was only the boy he wanted. But where had he been all these years, she wanted to know. That was none of her business, Ted Grimsley answered with some bitterness. "And your wife?" Cynthia asked him. The boy's mother had disappeared, she was told, but he now had a new wife who, like him, wanted custody of the child.

Cynthia O'Dea never forgot that phone conversation, the feeling of the phone melting in her hand, the sensation of her bowels exploding inside her, and the terrifying fantasy that was born seemingly from nowhere.

"At first I thought it was a dream. When you become a foster parent, at least when I did, you tell yourself, now remember, this isn't *really* your baby. You have to act like it is, but somewhere in your mind you have to tuck away that minor little fact that another woman gave birth to this baby. She maybe didn't want it, but it *was* hers. But after a while that notion disappears and the child is really yours. So when all of a sudden the telephone rings and a man you've never heard of says *your* child is really *his* child, it's like someone hit you on the head with a hammer. I say I never heard of Mr. Grimsley, but of course I did. Not by name, but somewhere in my head I knew there was a father of this child. And if he wasn't dead, I told myself, it was very possible that someday he'd find out about his child. You read about these things happening in magazines.

"You know what I wanted to do? Invite the man over, give him a nice cup of coffee, you know, and a big piece of cake. Treat him so nice he'd say to me, 'You know Mrs. O'Dea, you and your husband are really so nice to this little boy you call Johnny, I don't have the heart to take him away from you. It's not even for his sake, but for your sake too. You're all such nice people here, I just can't see doing it to any of you. I don't know what got into my head.' Then I'd give him another piece of cake, a bigger one this time, maybe wrap up the whole cake and make him take it home with him. Then I thought, maybe the man could be a friend and we could tell Johnny it was really his uncle. Lots of families do that. The real parents, after a while, they change their minds, they want their child back. But lots of them will settle for being close so they can watch the child grow up. Child never knows, but I always think he suspects. Somehow you have the feeling *that* one must be my real mother. I bet she is.

"A foster child is always looking for real parents. That's something I believe very strongly. No matter how much you love them and take care of them, they have two questions buried in their minds: Why did my real parents give me up, and where are they? They'll tell everybody, as though it didn't bother them at all to talk about it, 'These people I live with, they ain't my real folks. My real folks are dead.' Real tough, like none of it mattered to them in the slightest. But they're thinking, 'My mother must know where I am; she's chasing me down, staying close. And she'd want to talk to me, so it's got to be someone I know, someone who made a special effort to move close to me.'

"I had another thing I imagined too, when Mr. Grimsley called. I imagined he took my cake and my coffee, and then with a nice big smile on his face told me I was the nicest person in the world he had ever met but it wasn't going to stop him from getting custody of his child. So then I slip into the kitchen, grab my biggest bread knife—my husband sees perfectly everything I'm doing but doesn't try to stop me 'cause he wants the same thing I do—and I come back into my living room smiling the same way I was when I went out, and when this Ted Grimsley isn't looking, I go up behind him and stick this ten-inch blade right smack into his back, on the left side too so I'll hit his heart. And you know what, doing it doesn't seem to bother me at all. Not in the slightest."

Happily for the O'Deas, the social service organization with which they had been working took immediate action with Ted Grimsley. They spoke with him hours after he had made his first contact with the O'Deas and explained to him the nature of the case. He had lost rights to the custody of his son, he was advised, and while he certainly could retain a lawyer to fight the court's ruling, it was doubtful that any judge would take Johnny away from the O'Deas, who were turning out to be ideal parents. Furthermore, in light of the many difficulties the boy had already sustained, it seemed wise for the state of his mental health to let him alone and not be burdened with more legal negotiations and the fear that once again he was to be shipped off to another family.

Ted Grimsley took in all the information quietly, not revealing his reactions to any of it. For several months there was no word from him and the O'Deas breathed easier. Then a letter came from a lawyer indicating that Mr. Grimsley had decided to take the custody case to court. After eight months of negotiations, conferences, and long telephone conversations, the case came up before the judge. Surprisingly, Ted Grimsley did not show up for the decision. He left word that his lawyer was to handle everything for him. The judge heard the testimony and continued the case for one week, while he read through psychologists' and teachers' reports. It was a harrowing week for the O'Deas, particularly for Peter, who, while he seemed to play a minor role in the proceedings, was becoming increasingly upset by the custody battle. Cynthia reacted directly to the hourly news from her lawyer and the social workers. When they brought encouragement, she went easily about her business. When a snag came up or a report seemed to indicate something negative, she wept openly and found herself unable to do her chores. What angered her more than anything was that throughout the eight months prior to the hearing, Johnny O'Dea lived in their house as their son. No matter what the judge might say, who was noticing, Cynthia repeatedly asked, that she and Peter were still parenting? Day in, day out, the lawyers were bickering and the social workers were interviewing people and filling out their reports. But who was keeping track of the hour-by-hour parenting that the O'Deas were doing so well that, as far as anyone could tell, neither Johnny nor Rosie knew anything about the custody fight? Still, with all the anger, Cynthia did have some calm and hopeful days.

Peter, on the other hand, was suffering in a way that no one fully appreciated, if they even noticed the intensity of his moroseness. The anger he must have felt never surfaced. It was not exactly that he took the matter personally; no one ever heard him speak against Ted Grimsley. It was a fact of life, he would say. It's natural for a father to want his son back. Everybody's always thinking about what children and mothers mean to one another, but not too many people think about what fathers feel about children, even when their children are not their own biological children. Perhaps this was part of his somber mood, the feeling that nobody recognized his role, his hurt, the humiliation and terror that *he* was feeling. It was as if he had two purposes in life: making money so nobody had to worry about housing, clothes, food, doctor bills; and supporting his wife and children in a human way, but not so much that he would become the number one person, for this was his wife's position. He was not meant to be forgotten or overlooked, but his role kept him in the background. Peter O'Dea said it plainly: "I'm always in the shadows. They know I'm here but they can't quite make out my face. But it's always all right because they know I'll be here following them around like their shadow."

In the eight months of waiting and preparing for the trial, Cynthia O'Dea carefully watched the moods and behavior of her nine-year-old son and five-year-old daughter. She spoke to their teachers and learned that the children were doing fine in school; there were no problems to report. She did not observe her husband that carefully, although she knew he was deeply troubled by the custody fight. She could not know, of course, that whatever was eating away at Peter would not disappear after the final judgment had been issued. The facts of his own background, of her own background for that matter, were not relevant at this time. Peter felt the same, at least he said he did. Everything in their lives now took a back seat to the most serious matter they had ever encountered: the possibility that they might lose custody of their son.

As it happened, the social workers' predictions proved absolutely right. The judge saw no reason for the boy legally named Johnny O'Dea to live with anybody but Peter and Cynthia. His nine years had been hard enough, and the O'Deas, by all reports, were proving to be perfect parents. Reports from everyone showed his development, both physical and mental, to be excellent, hence there was no reason to warrant a reevaluation of the foster home situation. And, the judge concluded, looking straight at Cynthia O'Dea, the parenting behavior of Cynthia and Peter O'Dea during the ordeal of the last eight months was not only honorable; given its nature, it was unbelievable. "You don't like the reports the social workers make," the judge said to Cynthia, "but I'll bet you're happy they made monthly reports on *you* these last eight months." Cynthia nodded and wept. She barely saw Peter's happiness. Mr. Grimsley's lawyer looked perfectly stoical. That he lost the case seemed to matter not at all to him. Cynthia commented later that he looked like a man who wanted a *Time* magazine and was told they were sold out so he bought *Newsweek* instead and never knew the difference.

How they celebrated that night—the O'Deas, two of the social workers, and some friends. Johnny and Rosie could not understand the celebration but they couldn't care because each received lovely presents and it wasn't even Christmas or their birthday. Peter too seemed happier than he had in years; he was outright effusive. He bought a box of cigars and offered them to everyone he saw, men and women alike, and everyone took one because they knew he was at last announcing the birth of his children. That he did not smoke and only chewed on one of the wrapped cigars only made the celebration that much more delicious.

Within the year, Peter O'Dea would be dead, a suicide victim at thirty-eight. The celebration ended quickly for him. He worked, met his responsibilities, but never seemed able to pull himself out of the slump into which he had fallen. He admitted to some friends at work that his feelings were becoming very heavy. It was like extra pounds he couldn't lose no matter how he dieted. They urged him to take a drink now and again. Lots of men take a couple at lunch and at dinner to sort of pull themselves up, he was told. It didn't make anyone an alcoholic. But Peter O'Dea was a man who never drank, never smoked, never even swore. He claimed he had nothing against people who did, it just wasn't his style. It also wasn't his style to complain or reveal his feelings, even when he could barely conceal them.

On a cold February night with the snow piled high around the O'Dea home, Peter went quietly into the backyard. He told Cynthia he was going out to check on something. They had been watching television together and he had been falling asleep in his usual manner. She never knew about the sleeping pills he had swallowed. She found the bottle in the garage. Outside in the small yard behind the house, he shot himself, the bullet entering his right temple. The police later found an envelope on the garage floor. On it was written, "To be opened in the event of my death." The envelope was not sealed; it contained nothing.

Rosie O'Dea had been awakened by the shot and the noise and crying that followed. Johnny slept through everything until his mother decided he had to be roused. Strangely, he recalled that he had been dreaming of a large bear wearing a suit and a tie just like a real man. The bear had been walking on a street in the city. Nobody had taken notice of the bear except for one person who was afraid the bear might bring harm to the people in the city. The person went immediately to a store and bought a big gun and shot the bear. Then everybody ran up to the person and yelled and screamed at him for shooting the bear. The person was frightened and began to cry until someone took the suit off the bear and said, "It's a bear. It could have killed us. This person has done a great thing. Now we're all saved!"

Johnny O'Dea did not see the body of his father being covered with a blanket, placed on a stretcher, and taken away. He was looking out the kitchen window when the police officer kicked the snow where his father had died, trying to cover up the blood. In the morning, when it was light, Johnny went into the yard and dug in the snow where the policeman had been working. It wasn't hard to find the traces of his father's blood. He remembers the snow, gray with dirt, and the patches of reddish-brown. He remembers, too, hunching up his shoulders as though saying, well that job's over, and going to his mother and asking, "When is Daddy coming back? In time for my birthday?" Peter O'Dea had died four days before his son's tenth birthday.

The next two years were difficult ones for Cynthia O'Dea. They were filled with a lingering sadness, a profound sense of loss, and an underlying feeling of guilt she could not shed, no matter what she said or did. She invested a great deal of time speaking both with her minister and the social worker who had helped in the custody fight. But nothing helped her. She had persuaded Peter never to tell anybody about his mother's suicide when he was fourteen. It would have ruined their chances, she said, of ever adopting children. Peter had agreed, but then went on to argue that Cynthia not only denied the fact of his mother's suicide, but turned away as well from his problems, his depression. Cynthia had said that she could not be that sympathetic to her husband when she herself was depressed about not being able to have children. Then, when Johnny and Rosie were safely and legally in their home, she had no time to take much interest in Peter. He told her he had lost both ways. While a source of joy, the children were not making up for his constant sadness.

Then too, Cynthia had to admit that even while mourning for her husband, she found herself thinking about the children, especially Johnny, and feeling furious at Peter for what he had done to *them* by killing himself. She had always said that the children come first, particularly these children who had sustained so much in such a short time.

Peter had talked about suicide so often, Cynthia admitted to the social worker, she had long ago ceased taking interest in it. She never made an issue of it, even when Peter announced six months before he killed himself that he had purchased a gun. She was frightened by his news but again, her thoughts turned immediately to the effect his death would have on the children. "You live for them," he had said that night. "Just for them," she had responded, well aware that she was purposely letting another opportunity to discuss his depression slip away. But nothing must ever happen, she pledged, to jeopardize the fostering of her two children.

By eleven years of age, Johnny O'Dea had lost all the gentle, naive quality that had endeared him to people. As friends of the O'Dea family would report, the only lovely quality he had kept from childhood was his beautiful skin. For the first time he was becoming a problem in school. He had begun to hang around with older boys, and if he wasn't getting into a fight with someone, then he was trying to start one. He was unable to keep friends and was barely managing to do enough work in school to pass his courses. His teachers were predicting the worst for him. While everyone who knew him or had the slightest information about his background felt compassion for him, they could barely stand to be with him. He was always in one of two moods, sullen to the point of silence or angry to the point of being openly insulting and combative. He saw nothing wrong in swearing at a teacher or yelling at a policeman, and anyone who tried to calm him when his anger rose up was likely to get hit or spat upon. That his mother had been forced to move the family into a less expensive apartment after his father's death did not help the boy's morale. Nor did the fact that he had to transfer schools. Nor the fact that his mother had begun to drink.

By thirteen, Johnny O'Dea had convinced himself that toughness was the only valuable quality; in his world, it was money. He loved telling people he didn't care what happened to him and that he wasn't afraid of anybody. He'd even go into a fight that was patently unfair if he felt in the mood.

Johnny O'Dea was arrested for arson when he was thirteen and a half. He was taken to jail in a paddy wagon. Inside the wagon he fought with another boy who had been arrested with him. At the police station where he was booked, he scuffled with a policeman who was pinning his arm back. For this he spent two days in solitary confinement. On the day he was released from solitary, he was arraigned in court and set free on one thousand dollars bail. Despite the unnecessary punishment of solitary confinement, the case of Johnny O'Dea might have ended when the court released him, except that his forty-eight hours in a cell by himself, without light and sound, had an effect on him which never wholly subsided.

Shortly after being released, he developed a tic on the right side of his face, and weeks later he began to stammer slightly. In addition, a fear of heights and closed spaces developed into phobias. He insisted on sleeping with the light on and refused to ride in the back of a car if he was crowded by other people.

"I can barely think about those two days," Johnny O'Dea once said. "Those tall walls coming in on me, me standing there looking up at that ceiling like it was coming down on top of me inch by inch. And it was wet in there; like I was sweating, you know, and there wasn't nowhere for the sweat to go so it just stayed in there with me. Then it got hot, then it got cold. Holy God, it was the worst thing I ever knew about. I'd touch the walls and they'd be cold one minute and maybe hot the next. Like, I couldn't tell no more what I was feeling. They didn't give me no bed to sleep on. They didn't even have no toilet. They had like the top of this sewer pipe sticking up out of the floor and you had to piss and shit in it. And you couldn't see, so you'd be reaching around in all that darkness hoping you'd find it, and hoping you wouldn't put your hands in anything at the same time. It smelled. I was walking around in my own piss there. I got so afraid I just walked to a corner to take a piss. I didn't know what was wrong with me. I wouldn't go find the pipe no more. I'd just do it and the damn stuff drained down the floor, you know, stinking up the place.

"Then they gave me this lousy food. I didn't even eat it. I was afraid. I could barely see the stuff. How'd I know it wasn't filled with bugs and ants? I didn't think they'd poison me or nothing. I was just afraid maybe all these bugs would get in the food and I wouldn't see 'em. If I ate the stuff and threw up, which I knew I'd do, I'd have to smell that stuff in there, too. So I didn't eat or drink nothing for the whole two days.

"I can still see that room, man. I can feel those walls and how hard they were. They wouldn't put a sick dog in one of those cells, but they had no problem sticking me in there, and lots of guys before me and after me too. I kept thinking, maybe someone's dead in here with me. Maybe on the floor somewhere I'm going to find a body of some kid just like me who they stuck in there once and he never got out. I'm going to find a body in there, man. I can feel it in here. I *know* it's in here somewhere. So I ain't moving from this spot. I ain't going nowhere 'cause if I trip on it that'll do me in. I mean, I ain't going to live after finding it.

"You see how I'm talking about it? I'm talking about those two days like they was still happening, instead of being like two years and two months ago. I hope I never have to go back in there. I'd kill myself first. I'd find some way to do it, believe me. Then the next guy who goes in there afraid he's going to stumble over somebody, he will. He'll fall over me and land on that cold hard miserable floor."

If the time in jail had a deterrent effect on Johnny O'Dea, no one saw it. Less than two weeks after being released from jail he was again in trouble. This time he was caught with three girls, stealing a car. He claimed he had had sex with all of them, and then, looking for something to do, he decided to take an automobile. When the police chased him down he threw a brick through the car's front window, then calmly reached his hands out in front of him making it easy for a policeman to put the handcuffs on him. The girls with him were bewildered by his behavior. They told the police it had been Johnny's idea to steal the car although they had not protested. As for the sex, they denied it, claiming that Johnny O'Dea had never had sex with anyone and wouldn't know what to do with a girl if he had a book of instructions in bed with him.

For the car theft, Johnny O'Dea was sentenced to jail for a period of time not to exceed one year. In jail this second time he became known as the punk, the boy who'd put his hand through a brick wall if nobody was around to fight. One of the older inmates, a twenty-year-old man named Joey Hathaway, claimed he had sized up Johnny O'Dea the moment the boy entered his cell. Joey Hathaway is a strong, athletic man with long, blond hair that he combs, seemingly every other minute.

"Kid comes in here, I knew that kid like I knew myself. I see two things second he turns toward me. I see the way he carries his hands. He's a fighter. Angry guy, too much anger for a kid his age. Either he's never had the shit kicked out of him, or he's angry about things that he doesn't even know about. That's the way I figured from his hands. Second thing I see is the way he screws his face up, you know what I'm talking up. That little tic of his. I see that, I tell myself, okay, it's one of two things, maybe both. The kid's been in jail before, although he sure looked kind of young to be a con already. His skin makes him look a lot younger than he is. Either that, or he's seen death, someone dying, you know what I mean, and it made him upset. That's what I figure from the way he screws his face up.

"When you're outside and you're walking around and you see people and they got a funny thing they do with their face, you laugh at them 'cause they look funny to you, or you don't notice 'cause you ain't thinking that much about it. But in here all that changes. All your learning goes on in *here* when you've been here as long as I have. Twenty years old, I'm here or someplace like it on and off since I'm ten. You want to know what I did when I was ten? Don't tell nobody or they'll take me out of here and put me on death row. When I was ten years old—now you got to promise you ain't going to tell nobody—I cut school. Terrible, ain't it? I should feel lucky all I got was a little time in the can, huh? I mean, if I hit the wrong judge, Jesus, maybe they would have shot me. I mean a kid ten years old who cuts school for a couple months and sits in the goddam gutter near his home shooting marbles—that's what I did too, shot marbles—he's a goddam menace to society, ain't he? Person isn't safe in the street anywhere in this country with a ten-year-old marble shooter sitting in the goddam street picking his ass all the time 'stead of sitting in a boring goddam school somewhere.

"So you get my point. They don't teach you nothing in here like in school, so you learn the whole world from the people you see. I see little Mr. O'Dea walking in here with his tic, I'm thinking what he is, who he is. I see those eyes of his, I say to myself, all right, point number one, the kid's an orphan. All right? That's the first thing I see. World's got two kinds of eyes. Not brown and blue, like most people see. Eyes that could be happy if a kid wasn't facing life in here and eyes that ain't going to be happy no matter what anybody does. They don't sizzle no more. That's my word for it. O'Dea's eyes, they don't sizzle; they didn't sizzle the second I saw him; they never did.

"Now you got that tic. Two kinds of people in the world: Guys with screwed-up faces and normal guys. Guys with the screwed-up face, they got anger pushing 'em in one direction, fright pushing 'em in another direction. They saw something or felt something they didn't like, didn't like at all. Something really hit 'em hard, harder than they could take, although they don't know that at the time. Maybe they saw someone die. Or maybe they got hurt in a fight. Lots of guys are really frightened when they do their little criminal number that gets 'em a nice cozy place in here. You read about them, and you always got all these people saying they're psychopaths, they don't have a conscience, nothing telling 'em they shouldn't be doing what they're doing. Maybe that's true, although I never met a person young or old like that. Everybody's got a conscience. It's just that when somebody's getting into trouble he don't think, what if I get caught, what if I get caught? He thinks, so *what* if I get caught, what have I got to lose? Just my poverty, baby. Just my poverty. People got consciences, all right. They're thinking about all sorts of things. But they're scared, man. Oh are they ever scared. Not of being caught maybe. Not of being anything in particular, maybe. Nobody has *ever* told me what it's all about. But they are scared. And when a man gets scared often enough it's going to show. He ain't going to hide it, 'specially from the type of guy you find in here. It's got to show through. He'll bullshit you, he'll bullshit himself 'til he's green in the face, but he'll never hide it forever. You ask O'Dea, 'You scared, man?' He'll tell you, 'Hell no. Scared of who? What for, man?' But all the while he's talking his face is twitching away, talking to you in another language and it's saying, you bet your ass I'm scared.

"They got another thing though that gives guys a tic. It's an old deal; they call it jail. I see O'Dea twitching like that, and like I said, all this is going through my mind in the first minute I see him, I tell myself, he looks young, he looks like he's been the king of a territory no bigger than twenty yards, 'cause you can see he ain't got no experience marks on him, but that kid's been behind bars. He's been in here before, or somewhere. Kid's got jail marks on him. Solitary maybe. Solitary or some son of a bitch sadistic guard beating him in the gut one day or making him pile dirt from one spot to the other, that'll make you have a twitch in your face that nobody's going to take out for you. Kid's tough. Believe me he's tough. But he was tough before he came in here. He was going to fight anybody—the guards, the inmates. Hell, he might come into the visiting room some day and pick a fight with someone 'cause he doesn't like what they're wearing. First day he was in here, very first day I ever saw the kid, didn't even know his name, I see him in this room they got here with the guys playing cards. He couldn't have been in there five minutes. Came in here in the morning. So I go up to him and I say, like, 'What do you say, kid?' So the kid goes, 'I don't say much of nothing, but it looks like you can't say the same about you.' Didn't even know the guy and he's toughing it out on me. So you know what I did? I hit him so hard on the side of the head he had to go to the hospital have 'em put stitches in there. I didn't want to do it, but kids like that, no matter how hard they're hurting, or from what, sometimes you got to let 'em know what they can and can't do. You think that helped him? You think he apologized to me the next time he saw me, or stayed away? Never. Next time I saw old peaches-and-cream skin, he's starting all over again with me. Nothing good coming out of his mouth. So I recognized right away he's got this problem about being close to people, you know. Kid like that's going to make it a practice to stay away from people. I told him, 'Fuck with me I'll send you to the hospital all over again.' He don't mess with me now, but we ain't that good friends either. He don't want friends. Well, maybe he does, he just don't know how to get friends and what to do with 'em if he has 'em.

"So what do you say about a guy like John O'Dea. First thing you say is the worst place for him in the world is jail. That's the worst place. Couldn't be worse. And you know he's going to be put in solitary, sooner or later, or punished, 'cause the guy can't go two days without finding some kind of trouble. Kid's destined, you know what I mean? Destined. Second thing is you know jail is the worst place for him and that's where he's going to end up, eight years out of ten. He'll get out of here, but he'll be right back in some place. I'll give him no more than six months. Six months tops and he's behind bars. I know it. Nothing big, he'll never do nothing really big. He'll just keep coming back every once in a while 'cause he can't make it out there, and he can't make it in here, so he's got to travel around. He's like a guy on the run, fugitive, you know what I mean? He ain't got a home and he never will. And you know when that toughness of his will wear off? Ten days after his soul leaves him. I mean that guy's going to his grave tough. He'll go to hell tough and toughen up the folks down there too before they start shoving him around. Although if he keeps having the luck he's been having, they'll probably tell him he ain't got no home there either. I pity the son of a bitch. I really do. I sort of want to be a friend, like an older brother to him. Maybe someday when we're both out of here I'll meet him in the street, you know, and we'll talk, you know, and I'll try to help him, and he'll get tough in his way and I'll break his face open for him. Maybe scratch up that lily-white skin of his a little. Think that'd help? I doubt it. What he needs right now is for his mother to quit drinking and show him a little of the old love she ought to have left in her."

Joey Hathaway, the man they called the inmate's shrink, saw his predictions borne out. Johnny O'Dea was released from prison after serving seven months of his one-year term and was back behind bars five months later. This time he had not only stolen a car, but four cases of bourbon as well, which had been taken from the basement of a liquor store. Only a couple of friends went to court with him. Cynthia O'Dea promised to go but she did not put in an appearance. Johnny told the two friends who did come that his mother was probably drunk. His friends said something important came up. "I don't give a shit one way or the other," he grumbled. "I'm going back to jail so what do I give a fuck. Rather be there than school anyway."

Sentenced to jail for a slightly longer period of time than before, Johnny O'Dea stood in the courtroom facing the judge as though he hadn't heard a word. There was nothing defiant in his posture; he was not refusing to listen. Rather, it seemed that he was in a trance. He stood perfectly still; not even his chest moved as he breathed. Strangely, too, he seemed at peace, although his eyes, as Joey Hathaway would have observed, were hardly sizzling. He remained this way throughout the ride to prison and for the next several days. It was clear that he was not only turning inward in a manner no one had ever seen in him, but that he was terribly preoccupied with something.

Within a week in prison he resumed his old ways and found himself engaged in fights, one of them a bloody brawl in which Johnny knocked out three teeth of his adversary, a man named Tullings. Apparently, Tullings had teased Johnny about knowing his real father. At first Johnny had been interested. Then, on realizing that a malicious joke was being played on him, he struck out at Tullings and ripped the man's mouth open with his fist. Both men were placed in solitary confinement for several days, and a prison psychiatrist was instructed to examine Johnny who, the guards contended, was on his way to committing murder.

On three occasions Johnny O'Dea sat with the psychiatrist, an hour each time. He said not one word, and nodded his head only to the question, "Are you comfortable?" Each time he walked in, sat down, and stared down at the floor. Nothing the psychiatrist did or said could provoke a response of any sort. Toward the end of their third hour, after the psychiatrist had asked him whether there was anything he could do for Johnny and the boy still refused to speak, the psychiatrist announced he had reached the limit of his patience. Since Johnny was not going to communicate, there was no reason for the two of them to meet any longer, the psychiatrist said. Johnny O'Dea stood up, walked past the psychiatrist, and headed for the door. He opened it slowly, then turned to speak for the first time. He would later explain that his turning to speak just before leaving was modeled after a scene he had seen in a movie. It could not have been less genuine. But what he said was truthful. The doctor had helped him. A lot.

"But how exactly did I help?" asked the psychiatrist, surprised that the boy would even bother to open his mouth, much less believe that their hours of silence could have meant anything to him.

"Because," Johnny began cautiously, "it's the first time in my life anybody just sat with me and didn't force me to say nothing or do nothing. You just let me think about what was in my head."

"And what was that?" the psychiatrist asked quietly, willing to let the meeting last as long as Johnny wished.

Johnny O'Dea waggled his finger at the doctor and broke out into a smile. "You're going to ruin it, doc," he said. "Let's just let it go."

One week later Johnny and three other inmates were involved in a fight. No one could discover the cause of it. Before anyone even began punishment proceedings, Johnny announced in his toughest voice, "All right, bring in the solitary cell. I don't give a crap where you put me." One of the guards, for whom Johnny had no love at all, was only too happy to oblige, and when word came down that O'Dea was to go to solitary, off they went.

Paul Bucconi had worked as a guard in this one prison for five years. During that time he claimed he had seen some of the toughest boys and men in the state. He never analyzed them, he said. There was rarely enough time for that. In Johnny O'Dea he saw what he called the saddest kid he'd ever seen in his life. He said, too, he wanted to be caring and develop some kind of a trust relationship with the boy, but Johnny wouldn't let him get close. Not only that, Johnny became like a tiger when someone tried to approach him, until at last Paul Bucconi, despite his efforts to control himself, had grown to dislike Johnny. He found himself hoping that Johnny would either get himself beaten up in a fight so badly he'd never open his vile mouth again or that he, Paul, would have a chance to mete out some punishment to him.

For weeks they had played the same cat-and-mouse game: Paul watching for Johnny to break some rule, Johnny watching Bucconi watching him, teasing him with his good behavior. And both men were fully aware of their own and the other man's thoughts, but not letting themselves express a concern for the other. Then came the fight, and Paul Bucconi seemingly had his chance to stick it to the boy with the pretty skin. He marched Johnny O'Dea across the small prison yard, through one building and out of it at the other end, across a large yard where a group of men stood around taking a rest from their work in the kitchen and laundry, and then into the building where the men sentenced to solitary confinement were housed.

"I was watching the kid very closely," Paul Bucconi reported. "I was studying him. I didn't think he was about to start trouble, it was just that I had to study him for some reason. He was strutting away with that walk of his where he's got to show the world how tough he is, and I'm thinking, you're the biggest liar, O'Dea, I've ever seen in my life. Whatever happens to you it won't change you. I don't know whether you're really scared or tough or what and I'm not certain I really care all that much. I never *did* anything illegal with him, but I'll admit I'd gotten to the point where I couldn't stand the sight of him. Honest to God. But there was something about him that I couldn't put my finger on. Some quality about him that kept getting me angrier and angrier, and yet, I suppose, feeling sorry for him. But the more I felt sorry for him, the more I got angry at him for what he was doing to my feelings. I can't say it right but you know what I mean.

"So here we are, just the two of us, walking him to the solitary cell, and he's strutting like someone was making a movie of him. It was like the scene where the guards walk the prisoner to the electric chair and you're sitting in the movie wanting to yell, 'But he's innocent. He's innocent.' I swear to God, that's exactly what it was like. He made it like that for himself, everything a scene out of a movie as if he were acting his way through life. Maybe that's what he wanted to do. Maybe that's the only way he could handle all the horrible stuff that happened to him. He'd had it tough too. Lots of men in here, in jail everywhere, have had it tough. Not all of them. You'd be surprised. Lots of these guys, you find out about them, what their background is like and you can't figure why they'd suddenly go get a gun and shoot someone. It doesn't always figure so easily. Oftentimes, it's easy for the person on the outside who doesn't know these guys to make their theories about why one guy gets into trouble and another one doesn't. But when you get to know them like we do in here, very little makes sense. Sometimes it makes a nice picture. Broken home, someone's died, there's alcoholism, orphanages, the usual. We know a little about that and we *say*, well, that guy I can understand, look at his past. But then you get people from the same background who don't end up like these guys. You can't say that everyone from a broken home is automatically on his way to jail. I was an orphan and put into two different foster homes with the weirdest bunch of people you've ever seen in your life. I don't have the slightest idea to this day who the hell my real parents were. And man I tried for years to find them, either one of them. I'm still looking. I still write to people, orphanages, lawyers' offices. You know that once I paid a private investigator a hundred bucks to track down a lady who claimed she knew where my father was. Out of the blue this guy I had been in contact with wrote me and said there was a lady who knew my father. So I paid this guy to find her. A hundred dollars. I never saw him again, the money, the lady, nothing.

"So you can say, guys like us, from where we come from, *what* we come from I suppose is more accurate to say, we either become prisoners or their custodians. But that doesn't explain too much because what are you going to do with all these people from orphanages who are just regular guys now, never been in prison in their lives? Never got in trouble. You can't explain it. What you can say is that a kid like Johnny O'Dea makes believe he's much older than he is. Fact he does it so well you forget he's really a kid. Not only that, he's a kid who's never had any of the good times most kids have, so he spends all his time either thinking about that or pretending there's nothing wrong with him or the way he was brought up. And that's a problem too. There's one theory that says if horrible things happen to you, you repress them, keep them away from yourself. You don't think about them. What you're really doing is wishing they weren't there. Only you wish so hard they actually *aren't* there, at least you can't see them. Then another theory goes that kids like Johnny see all the horrible things happening to them, fathers, mothers, the whole routine, and decide it was *their* fault that all this stuff fell on their head. So they have to repress a lot of what went on because it was too painful for them to think they caused it.

"But I have another theory. My theory says they repress their lives, everything that's happened to them, because it's just too painful to think about. They know damn well they didn't have anything to do with the events that happened. O'Dea didn't arrange to have himself orphaned or fostered. He had nothing to do with his foster father's death. The man was sick a long time as I understand it. And he was only a little boy. His mother drinks for reasons that the kid wouldn't understand when he was small. So I say he represses everything because it hurts too much.

"Anyway, there we are walking into his cell where he's going to be and, like I say, I was glad to be putting him away. But he's there strutting all the way. He isn't going to let on he's got anything else on his mind but being the tough kid. So I shoved him into the cell. I remember because I was surprised when I touched the back of his shirt how sweaty he was. Second I opened the door we both smelled the inside of it. It smelled of urine; it was terrible, like it hadn't been cleaned in years. I tried to turn on the lights but they weren't working. The kid didn't turn around to look at me once. He knew what I was thinking, that with all my hatred for him I didn't have the heart to shove him into the room. I didn't have any idea of the conditions, the smell. Solitary's bad enough without a person's wastes on the floor. People aren't animals. And here I had someone who was still a boy. And what really had he done? Stole things which he never would be able to afford. You got a guy in for rape or murder, he's done something to somebody. But steal a car? You don't close your eyes to that but you don't kill a kid for doing it either. He knows right from wrong. A kid like O'Dea does. I know he does.

"When I pushed him into the cell he practically fell over on his face. He must have been surprised as hell I would do it. Then I slammed the door shut on him as fast as I could so I wouldn't have to see him or think about him. But I couldn't get myself to go away. I just stood there, like an idiot, hoping no one would come by and ask what I was doing. Part of the punishment is to not let them speak with anybody. Probably helps them to adjust to the new situation knowing they're alone. I wasn't standing there two minutes before I heard him in there crying like a baby and begging to speak to me. 'Mr. Bucconi, Mr. Bucconi,' he's calling me. 'Please open the door. Please open the door. I can't make it. I can't make it. I'm afraid. I'm so afraid.' And he's sobbing, you know. You could barely understand the guy. 'Mr.

Bucconi, Mr. Bucconi.' What do I do? I know for sure I didn't hate him anymore. Whatever I was feeling for the guy was washed away when I heard him crying. But my job was to put him away. And thirty seconds earlier I might have wanted to stick a knife into his back. The way he was walking with me through the yard it was like he was daring me to do it too. Like he was saying, come on, you coward, do it while I'm not looking. But now there he was crying, begging for me, like I was a schoolteacher. *'Mr. Bucconi,'* he was calling. Nobody calls me Mr. Bucconi. Nobody anywhere!

"So I opened the cell, and again that horrible smell of urine was there. The kid never mentioned it. That wasn't what was troubling him. I saw him on this filthy smelly tiled floor, like a bathroom, on his hands and knees, and he was praying. Tears coming down his face, soaked with perspiration which he didn't even notice, and he's praying. He's got his two hands up there, like he was in church. And the poor guy's face is twitching worse than I ever saw it. First time I met him I didn't notice it. I looked at the guy and he seemed all right. I noticed he had smooth skin, like a girl's. I thought maybe he was one of these sick types we get here all the time. Someone who's always combing his hair or cleaning his fingernails twenty times a day. We had a guy once insisted on brushing his teeth once every hour. Never chewed gum, ate very little, and he wants to brush his teeth every hour. And with all that he had the lousiest looking teeth of anybody in the whole institution. But O'Dea wasn't freaky like that. I saw the tic later on. He took a little bit of razzing about it, but most of the guys leave someone alone when they see something like that. You've got the occasional wise guy who yells out, 'Hey Blinkey, how are you Blinkey?' But they didn't do that so much with O'Dea. But that time his face was really going; I said to myself, the kid's praying and his face looks like a pinball game, all the lights flashing and the balls jumping around and the flippers, you know. I never saw anyone in the condition he was in that day in front of the solitary cell. He wasn't having a mental breakdown. He was as understandable as he could be. It was worse than that. If he'd been, like, mumbling to himself then I could have dealt with it better, but he was perfectly sane. And all the time he's calling for *me*. He knew exactly where he was, what was happening to him. He knew what was going on just as well as I did.

"So I knelt down. Felt like a priest doing it. I didn't even realize I was putting my arm around his shoulder. I didn't even feel him 'cause I certainly would have remembered how sweaty he was. I just looked at him and there was my arm lying over his shoulders. 'What's wrong?' I asked. He was whispering to me. Like he didn't have the energy even to speak out loud. 'I can't take it,' he says. 'Please don't put me in there.' It sounded like he was going to die right there, and I was thinking, this kid dies, everybody in this state is going to pin it on *me*! 'Cause I had told some people how I really didn't like him at all. 'I can't take it,' he keeps saying. A lot of guys, 'specially the younger ones, they always say this. Everybody's always begging for something. Promising you they're going to turn over a new leaf, and you know damn well they're going to be their same lousy selves in twenty-five minutes. But John O'Dea never said that. He promised nothing. There wasn't even a mention of how he was going to reform, how he'd seen the light. He didn't come up with any of that. He was just praying. He wasn't asking for forgiveness; he was just praying.

"I helped him up. I remember that. Here's this tough kid, one of the toughest boys this institution ever saw; certainly one of the toughest I ever knew, and I was helping him up as though every little bit of strength had fallen out somewhere on that smelly floor. If I'd let go he would have fallen down right on his head. I said to him, and I was still pretty tough myself, I have to admit it, 'What do you want? What am I supposed to do for you?' You know what the kid says? He says, 'I want something you can't give me. I want my father or my mother. My real father or my real mother. I need someone to help me look for them.'

"Well, like they say, the rest is history. I didn't know whether to laugh or cry. After all these years the guy decides he wants his mother or father. He told me later he'd been thinking about it for weeks. Ever since the trial when everybody thought he was in a trance, that's all he was thinking about. He said he spent hours trying to imagine what they looked like. He even took to drawing pictures of them, from his imagination, 'cause he'd never seen them. So there I was, holding up this kid. He's crying, I'm crying, 'cause I know what it's like not to know who your parents are and because I was so impressed that he didn't make any promises. He could have. They all do. But Johnny O'Dea probably never made a promise in his life. He knew that nothing he would want in this world would ever come to pass. I told him I'd help him. I got him out of solitary, made him my own responsibility. You know what he did? Behaved like the king of England for exactly two days. On the third day he was involved in a fight again. Somebody stopped him as he was about to throw a brick at some fellow. A cripple guy. But he'd won me over by then so I didn't care. I threatened him with solitary again and he behaved all right for another couple of days. Guy never belonged in jail. He needed help. Even if he just sat with a psychiatrist and didn't say a word, that would have been better. If he had the slightest chance of making it, even with that background of his, jail killed it. And that's the word I wanted to use. Kill!"

It took Paul Bucconi two months to find out about Ted Grimsley, Johnny O'Dea's real father. He learned from Mr.

Grimsley that Johnny's real mother had died several years before and that when he, Grimsley, got remarried, he had instituted the custody case. His new wife had encouraged him to go after the boy, which was something he had always wanted to do. It had been his lifelong dream to find Johnny and live with him again. He also had instituted proceedings to regain custody of another child, a girl, who was born a year before Johnny. Shortly after the custody case was settled in favor of the O'Deas, Ted Grimsley's wife walked out on him and went to live with another man and Ted Grimsley gave up any plans to have a family. He lost his job, took to drinking, and never again inquired about his son or daughter. He never even paid his attorney in full. The lawyer had accepted a small retainer, expecting to be paid later on, but after a year of trying to find Grimsley, the attorney gave up.

But Paul Bucconi found the man. One night very late he received a telephone call. A man, quite drunk and speaking from a bar, introduced himself as the man Bucconi was tracking: "I'm the animal you want, Mr. Bucconi." Paul Bucconi felt triumphant. He could not believe that it was now possible for him to bring the father and son together. It stirred up memories of his own childhood. When Ted Grimsley said he would visit Johnny in prison, Paul Bucconi cried. He cried the whole night, his wife Angela embracing him and weeping with him. The morning following the phone call Angela Bucconi telephoned her parents to tell them the story and they too were moved to tears. It's a story for the newspapers, Angela's father suggested. Maybe a reporter should be there when the father arrives. Paul put his foot down at the idea of publicity. He thought it best to allow the two men to meet in a private room rather than the public visiting room. He would make the arrangements himself.

When Johnny O'Dea heard what Paul had done he instinctively looked around to see whether anyone was observing him. Seeing he was alone with Paul he leaped into the air yelling as loudly as he could, "Holy fucking Jesus Christ. Holy fucking God! I'm going to buy you a dinner when I get out of here," he promised Paul. "I swear to God. We're going to have steak 'til it comes out of our fucking ears." Then for the first time in four months of friendship he asked Paul Bucconi a question about himself. "You got a family, Paul?" Paul Bucconi told him of his wife and four children. "I'm taking 'em all. Steak for everyone. And wine for your wife. I swear to God, I'll buy her flowers too. Do I get to kiss her?" Paul Bucconi nodded. "You're too loose with her, you jerk," Johnny teased him. "Let an Italian woman near an Irishman, she'll never look at you again." Johnny O'Dea laughed. It was the first time Paul had ever heard him laugh.

"You know what, kiddo, that's the first time I heard you promise anything except a whack in the mouth."

"Hey, you want me to promise that, I'll promise you that," John continued kidding his friend. "Your wife gets a kiss, your kids get steak and ice cream, and you, you get a whack in the mouth just like you ordered."

The two men stood in Johnny's white tile cell laughing. It seemed to Paul that Johnny O'Dea wanted to touch him, but he never let himself get close. Suddenly the laughing stopped and Johnny O'Dea was scratching his head in an exaggerated expression of puzzlement.

"Hey, you know before when I said that Italian women like your wife go for Irishmen like me? Well, how do I know your wife's Italian just 'cause you got an Italian name? That's question one. Question two is, if I don't know who my father is and who my mother is, how do I know I'm Irish? Jesus Christ! I could be a wop like you." He grinned at Paul.

"We wouldn't want you," Paul joked.

Johnny pretended he was going to punch him. "Jesus, now that it's happening, I'm not so sure I'm going to make it."

Paul Bucconi took a deep breath and dared to tell the boy an observation he had made. "You want to know something, man?" he began timorously. "Your face hasn't twitched since I told you the news. You know that? It hasn't moved."

Johnny O'Dea looked at the floor. "I know. I felt it stop, like a motor going off when you said my dad was coming."

Ted Grimsley was to arrive at the prison between two and four o'clock, regular visiting hours. Paul Bucconi promised to meet him on the front steps of the main administration building. Johnny O'Dea would be excused from afternoon classes and duties and would wait in his cell for word of his father's arrival. The story of the meeting of father and son had not spread throughout the prison, but a few of the men had heard about it. Johnny had told more people than he ever imagined he would, and they responded with warmth.

The afternoon finally came, the hours of the day dragging on for both Paul and Johnny. It was worse than any classroom he had ever been in, Johnny remarked to the boy in the cell adjoining his. Two o'clock came, three o'clock, and then visiting hours were over. Ted Grimsley never arrived. He never telephoned; he never wrote. Paul broke the news to Johnny who lay down on his bed. "I knew he wouldn't come, the chicken-shit son of a bitch."

Paul Bucconi would say later that if he ever found Ted Grimsley, he would kill him. It was hard enough trying to tell Johnny that he had learned that his mother had died. He could find no way to tell the boy how Grimsley's interest in his son fluctuated with his love life. And now he was unable to locate either Grimsley or the man who had led him to Grimsley in the first place. Ted Grimsley had disappeared exactly as Johnny O'Dea always said he expected his father would.

"Well, sir," Johnny told Paul the day he left prison for the second time. "You did the best you could. I lost my face for a couple weeks, even had a little hope going for me there for the first time in my life. I owe it to you. I guess *you'll* just have to be my father now. 'Cept no Irishman would ever take no Italian to be his father."

Paul Bucconi answered spontaneously: "But Italians take Irish for their sons. Any time you like, man, my home is open to you. Let me see you there, but not here. Can you promise that?"

"No way," came the reply.

"What you going to do?"

"I'm going into the big, cold, dark world, my man, get something to eat, see my old lady, probably pick her up off the floor where she's lying in some drunken stupor, check up on my sister who hasn't written me no letter in six weeks—I don't even know if she's still living at home no more—than go looking for Pickwick the Great or that other dunce I used to go with, Stevie Wiley. Used to call him Stevie Wonder. Guy hated that. I loved razzing him. He'd get so embarrassed, you know, his fuckin' ears would turn red. Like lights on a train. Then after, I don't know. Maybe I'll visit you, you never know. Most likely I'll probably say something to some guy that'll piss him off so much he'll start a fight. Yeah, that's probably what will happen. I'll fight with someone, or rob some store, probably end up taking some crummy little car again. One way or another I'll see you again. I'll bet money on that."

Paul Bucconi reached out his hand to Johnny O'Dea, but the young man pushed it aside.

"Get out of here with that shit. I'll see you again. I'll call you some night, real late, like my old man did to you. From a bar. Like father like son. Ain't that it? Like father like son."

Ten months later, Johnny O'Dea was found dead in the

back seat of a stolen car. The car was filled with blood, the windows broken, the inside totally destroyed. A police coroner reported that the boy had not died instantaneously. Quite likely he lay wounded in the car as long as three days before expiring. His death came two months before his eighteenth birthday.

8

I Wonder If Anyone Who's Been in Here Ever Feels Free Again

Beedie Helzer has one favorite topic: her friendship with Tina Korane, a girl she has known all her life. Sisters could not have known each other as well as these two fourteen-year-olds. To say that they were inseparable is an understatement. To those who knew them, they appeared to be attached to one another. If they went someplace to get a sandwich, they sat side by side in a booth. When one went to the lavatory, the other went right along with her. Even with boys they stuck so closely together it irritated their friends, as if that mattered to the two of them. They were friends, they would say when someone challenged their desire to be together. What are friends for if they can't be together when they want to?

The closeness of the two girls never disturbed their parents. Everyone considered it normal for teenagers to have close friendships even when others were excluded. That's just the way the young are, their parents said. Girls get girl friends, boys get boy friends. It doesn't have to lead to trouble. Actually Beedie Helzer's mother Irene and Tina Korane's father Michael were once childhood sweethearts and still saw quite a bit of one another. So several pleasant friendships existed between the families.

"It's very important that families stay together as long as they can," Irene Helzer once said, "because in this world there is every pressure one can imagine put on people to split up. It's very important for one family to get to know as many good families as they can so the children can grow up knowing that not all families end up destroyed with people running all over the place not knowing where their parents are, or their children are. It's very important. Especially with families like ours and the Koranes, families that don't have a great deal of money and never are going to have that much. Believe me, these children are very vulnerable. They're a bit like babies, not because they act like babies, but because the world is much more dangerous now than it's ever been. Nobody's safe. Not even the rich. What's this story I heard on the news a couple of weeks back where a football player from one of the colleges, a big fellow, over two hundred and thirty pounds, was attacked. A bunch of kids pulled him out of his car and beat him up. A big guy like that and they almost killed him. So what do I think when I have a fourteen-year-old girl walking around this city? Is she safe? Can I sleep at night knowing she's out somewhere? Can I tell her, 'Call me every time you go from one place to another'? Fourteen years old today isn't fourteen years old when I was young. These kids know so much more than we did it isn't funny. They're better kids too, because they have it harder. They're more vulnerable. There's danger every step they take. So if Beedie and Tina go together and are so close people wonder about them because with what's around for people to read and see on television, in the movies, everybody with a close friend has to be a homosexual, right, a lesbian, then my response is, with all the dangers in the streets, I'm glad they got each other, and to tell the truth I wish there were fifty of them that went around together!"

Kit Helzer, short for Kenneth, a man in his early forties, bald, with deep grooves in his forehead, thick lips, a man deeply proud of his zany sense of humor, could not have agreed more with his wife's sentiment. In the steel tubing plant where he had always worked, he was known as the man without worries. You had a problem, you went to Kit Helzer, because if Kit Helzer didn't have a joke or a song about the very thing that was troubling you, then nobody in the world could help you. His finest routines actually were on the subject of illness. If you came to him with a back pain or he noticed you were limping or looking glumly at a hand that obviously ached, he would regale you with stories, anecdotes, filthy jokes, or his own anxieties about illness. In minutes you were well, laughing, oblivious to any problems from your hurting back to your empty bank account to the news that your kid just flunked all his courses.

Beedie Helzer thought her father was more crude than funny. She rarely laughed when her father tried to be funny, especially when he used his wife as the butt of his jokes. But she couldn't always keep a straight face for he invariably had a way of getting to her. When she was small he loved to tickle her, but he gave this up when her body changed and she began taking on the appearance of a young woman. Then he would deluge her with jokes, all of which she had heard before. When that failed he would sing or dance or imitate the rock stars that Beedie liked so much. Tina would roar with laughter at Kit's antics, especially when he played the parts of an entire rock band he had seen on television. When Tina laughed, Beedie became less embarrassed about her father. She would see him as a special man, someone she could rely on. She would feel sad about the idea of growing up and moving away from her parents. Not far from them, probably, for it was doubtful that in her own life she would be more successful than they were, which meant richer. She was quite certain that she would end up marrying one of the boys she presently knew and settle down in the neighborhood. After all, how could she meet boys from other parts of the city, much less richer boys? And, if life merely repeated the same patterns as it surely had in her parents' case, then at least there would always be Tina.

Kit Helzer had no special plans or dreams for his three children. He wished them well, hoped their lives would be better than his, and tried not to think too much of what he had not done for them. As he always said, pressing problems pop up every day, just by a person being alive.

"I got a fourteen-year-old girl. Good-looking. Movie star? No, but she's all right. She's goddam all right and a body that could bother a whole lot of guys. Hell, I had her down at work several times and I could see these guys' mouths watering, tongues hanging out like a bunch of soldiers who hadn't seen a woman in years. And I happen to know these guys are seeing girls on the side, on the bottom, on the top, you know what I mean. These guys are doing it all the time. At home, at somebody else's home. All the time. So I know the girl is appealing to the opposite sex. Now that's fine, because while a father worries about whether his daughter's

good-looking and how she's going to be in the sexual sphere—
I mean, you don't want them messing around, you want to
keep them clean as long as you can—you also know it's a
dirty world, a very dirty world, and you got to change your
standards.

"You want to talk about a girl being a virgin 'til she gets
married? That's fine, I'll talk about that. But all that's
speculation. I got two statistics. One, I don't think anybody's a virgin on the night they get married. Two, I don't
know anybody doesn't cheat on their wife *and* husband.
Notice what I say: *and* husband. They used to talk about
how men cheat. Only men cheat. Right? So tell me, if it's
only men that cheat, where do they find all the women to
cheat with, if none of the women cheat? Either all the men
in the world are cheating with the same woman or they got
one helluva lot of women cheating. Huh? And they got a
helluva lot of men making out just fine with girls as young
as Beedie and Tina, who also isn't such a bad-looking girl.
All ages, all colors, all sizes, everybody's doing it. They got
all these debates on abortion. You got the right to have an
abortion, you got a law says you can. Then they got these
right-to-lifers. You get pregnant you have to have the baby.
You know what I think? I think it's all a lot of hot air.
People are doing it with each other by the billions. Every
day, every night. 'Round the clock. They're punching in all
over the place, all over the world 'round the clock. Fighting
it out on abortions is naive. Woman wants the baby, she'll
scream out against abortion. Six months later she's pregnant
again, she don't want this one, bang, she's screaming out *for*
abortions this time. When you got the problem, you're not
marching around on some picket line or making some big
political demonstration. You're either out buying baby furniture or you're looking for the best abortionist you can afford.

"I got a simple wish for my daughter and all her friends.
She should live a long life, keep her health, keep her job and

her husband, or get rid of both of them if they're unbearable, and have children only if she wants them. If she comes to me and says, I'm pregnant, you know what I do? I faint, that's what I do. Then I pick myself up off the floor and I look at her and I faint again. No, seriously, I look at her and I tell her calmly, 'Okay, kitten, you're pregnant; there's nothing so bad about that. Lots of people are getting pregnant every day. Most of them, they tell me, are women, and since that's what you are I'm not so disturbed by all this. Now you do one little thing for your nice old father who loves you so much. You just tell me the name of the nice little boy who did it to you and I shall go quietly to his home, introduce myself to his parents, and blow a nice little hole in his head with a rifle that I will go out and buy this minute!

"Nah, I'm only teasing. She gets pregnant, she makes the decision. Keep the child, have an abortion, put it in an orphanage. I'll support her right down the line. What am I going to do? Bring out a bunch of religious principles that were taught to me a thousand years ago that I didn't believe in when I heard them the first time and never taught to my own children? How can I be a hypocrite about it? It's all talk now, but it could happen. I know that. Irene knows it. The kid knows it. All these kids know the score. A girl like Beedie gets pregnant today, when she's only fourteen, what does she need a father to give her more grief? She wouldn't have enough trouble just being pregnant? Don't get me wrong, I'd have my views. I'd level with her. I wouldn't waste a minute telling her exactly how I feel about it. I got that right. She's my daughter and she's got to hear it. But once I tell her, I'm through. From then on, I support her. That's the secret of a family: caring for people. You always have the right to express your attitudes. You can't keep them bottled up inside you. They'll only explode. Believe me. I watched my father and mother holding on to their feelings. They didn't let out a drop of nothing. Because when all these feelings explode, they don't only kill the people standing right next to you, living in the same room with you. They hit everybody. So, first I tell her my feelings so there's no explosion, then I back her up.

"More important is that she's safe. You know what the biggest problem is about your kid getting pregnant? That they'll be ill? That they might die? Never. The biggest problem with your *kid* getting pregnant is everybody hearing about it and *you* feeling ashamed. That's your number one problem. *Your* shame, not what they've done. So right away in reaction to this feeling ashamed, people jump to two extremes. Either they disown their kid, pretend the kid doesn't exist at all, never did exist, or they jump the other way and decide there's absolutely *nothing* wrong with the kid getting pregnant. Monday morning they're running all over the place telling people how terrible it is all these kids thirteen, fourteen, twelve even, are pregnant or sick on drugs, right? Then Monday night their kid comes up to them and says, 'Daddy, I got news; I'm pregnant.' The guy's stunned, right? Has to be. His whole world has just been shaken, top to bottom. Preaches against pregnant girls and there he is with his own daughter pregnant. Tuesday morning here's this same guy running around the same places, telling the same people how he can't see nothing wrong with all these little girls his daughter's age being pregnant. Not a single thing in the world wrong with it. Twenty-four hours the guy's shifted all the way around 'til he's opposite to where he was the day before. 'Course that guy's a liar. Everybody can see it. He's conning everybody, especially himself. But the person he's hurting most is his own daughter, because she's going to pretend the same way he does. They're both getting into the act of believing everything is rosy. But inside, the both of them know they're lying, to themselves *and* to each other. It'd be much better in a scene like that for the father to come right out and tell his daughter exactly what he thinks. Don't beat around the bush or throw all your attitudes away 'cause something's happened which you couldn't possibly know was going to happen. You tell her plain and simple, then you help her. She knows where you stand; she knows you won't leave her.

"So, with that settled, Dr. Freud here has one more thing to say on the subject. If my daughter gets pregnant, I want it to be because she loved some guy and wanted to do it. Where we are in our civilization is not worrying about whether she gets pregnant, it's whether she gets raped! That's what you worry about. And you worry about it when they're seven and eight and nine, just the same way too. Perverts and maniacs everywhere. Guy rapes a woman, rapes three of them, and he may not be in jail. Or he goes in and he's out in a year, hornier and sicker than he was when he went in. Now he's hunting for seventy-year-olds as well as seven-year-olds. You think because Beedie runs around with Tina and a bunch of other girls most of the time that she's any safer? The hell she is. Everybody's vulnerable to something, but a fourteen-year-old girl who's even halfway good-looking is more vulnerable than anybody. Anybody can take her on for any one of a billion reasons, and all of them are going to bring trouble. All of them."

Between the families, the Helzers were known to be the noisy ones, the Koranes the quiet ones. Many of their friends were surprised that Irene Helzer had married Kit rather than Michael Korane, for she and Michael were less ebullient people, not shy, but hardly matches for the highly charged Kit. Madelaine Korane on the other hand, was like none of the others. A slight woman with a strong temper, she could also be tender and caring. But when her anger exploded she could be terrifying to those around her. It wasn't that she was mercurial or unpredictable. One had to push her hard to provoke the anger. She seemed to enjoy her life with

Michael, but there was little, actually, they did together. Things could have been better, but she was willing to accept what fate had handed her.

Michael Korane, in contrast, seemed to be growing increasingly bitter about his modest income and life-style. He never dreamed that he would have too much. Indeed what he had was about what he always imagined would be his, but it didn't suffice. He wanted more and hated the world and himself for not having it. He was suspicious of Madelaine always being so willing to accept the little that was theirs.

"I don't understand it," he would say when his frustrations no longer could be checked. "I don't understand why the woman has absolutely no ambition about her. I don't say you *have* to be the first at whatever you do, or live in the best house in the best community like some people seem to have to do. But you got to at least *know* about the best and try your damndest to get what you can. You don't blow your brains out when you fail, but you got to go for it, or as much of it as you can. But she goes around in life with that look on her face like whatever God puts in front of her, that's what she'll take. I don't get it. I've asked her ten million times to explain it, but she doesn't seem to want to try to understand it. It's like she believes the rich have all the advantages not just because they're rich but because they deserve it. Me, I say a lot of people just were born in the right hospital and spent the rest of their life going around as if they planned it to happen that way.

"She's going to explode, that woman. Some day she's going to take a good look around her and see how she's living, how her daughter's living, how the whole damn world is living, and she's going to sit up and take notice. Then you'll hear some screaming in this house. Then you'll see how she doesn't want to accept everything just because I have a little job with a little salary and not the slightest chance in hell of getting more. You'll see how she'll be when it dawns on her just what sort of life Tina and her brothers are heading for. You think these kids are going to be satisfied with a few thousand bucks a year? What do you think goes on in their minds when they walk around downtown looking in all these store windows where they're showing television sets and portable phonographs and tape recorders? I don't mean the real expensive things. I mean the little things a person with a reasonable income like us can buy. What do you think they think? They think, why can't all of us have an electric comb and a little portable radio and a TV set for our rooms and tape decks, the works? And how about a car, and every other year a new one? And what do they think when all the new products come out every year? Quadraphonic sound and all that stuff. Those kids will want a piece of the action.

"You know when they have those riots and those black families are yelling and screaming and burning down stores? I watch those people walk right in the front windows of those stores and take that stuff out of there, stuff they've wanted all their lives, and I sit there thinking, they got a right to it. Go take it for God's sake. Take as much as you can carry. You see these little kids weighed down with TV sets or Mixmasters. I say, take the damn stuff. Everybody else has appliances like those, why the hell shouldn't you? Hell, I'm sitting in a comfortable chair watching *them* on *my* television. Why shouldn't they be sitting in a comfortable chair watching somebody else get what *they* want? You'll see— Tina, Beedie, all of them, girls and boys, they'll want more. Wait 'til it dawns on them what school's preparing them for. The telephone company. Working in some boring, miserable office, getting coffee for a guy that makes more passes at you than he does anything else in his life. You think those girls like that? They hate it. Horrible work for horrible pay. And *that's* the best Tina can hope for. That's the top of the line. More likely she won't find work, or they'll stick her in some factory or some horrible place somewhere and she'll barely make enough, if they even have jobs to go around in a few years when she starts looking. Madelaine thinks everything's fine. She'll see. It'll dawn on her. You'll hear the explosion on the other end of the world. Probably cause a tidal wave on the far side of Australia!"

Michael Korane's prediction never came true. His wife had her infrequent blowups, expressions of anger usually at him or the children, but she remained a constant woman, able to bear up to the vicissitudes of a not wholly happy life. Michael, however, did not fare as well. By the time he reached forty he had become depressed, not so much that he lost his job, but enough that he made life unpleasant for his family. Surprisingly to his wife, he never drank. When he returned home from work, moping as was his custom, she made an effort to smell his breath. She tried to be inconspicuous about it, but soon he understood her actions. "Here!" he would shout, blowing his breath at her. "Do I pass the test tonight, officer, or do I go to jail? Am I disappointing you by not becoming an alcoholic?" His lateness was not because of stopovers in bars or late-afternoon visits with friends. He had lost interest in living. As there was little to come home to, he reasoned, why rush. The hurry of life was gone, vanished with everything else that he once held worthy. His wife was always the same, the routines of family life were always the same; nobody had any particular interest in him, so why hurry. For that matter, everybody was out of the house so much it was better to come home late for it increased the chances of finding someone at home. Even ten-year-old Matthew, the youngest child, was out every night until dark, despite his parents' orders and warnings. About the only thing interesting was the chance of a little visit with Tina. At fourteen, she was becoming quite attractive, and while Michael Korane knew of the dangers of fathers finding their daughters appealing, he could not deny the fact that he was stimulated by Tina. Every once in a while she would leave the door open when she was dressing or would run from the bathroom to her bedroom in little or no clothing and Michael would grow excited. Perhaps the most exciting moments were when Tina and Beedie would sit together listening to records. Michael would find them in provocative positions. In the summer they wore skimpy clothing, and often they danced together in their bathing suits. He would try to be secretive about his interests but he would spy on them. Tina noticed him when he prowled about, but she never said anything. She wanted to, but she was afraid. She never said anything about her father to Beedie. It was the first important matter she had ever kept from her friend.

Then, one autumn afternoon, Michael and Tina were alone in the house. Half-asleep on the living room couch, Michael caught a glimpse of his daughter walking into the kitchen wearing only her underwear. Suddenly driven by madness or a force he could neither understand nor control, he leaped up off the couch, ran to the kitchen, and began accusing his daughter of being pregnant. Terrified, Tina denied the accusation, calling him foolish and crazy. But Michael would not listen to her. He kept insisting that she had been with too many boys and must be pregnant. "I want to see for myself," he kept yelling. "Take down your pants, I'm going to see for myself." Tina tried to run away but Michael caught her, spun her around so that her back was pressed against his chest and then, as she screamed out, he pushed his hand inside her panties and ran his fingers over her genitals. By now, Tina could not move. She barely had the strength to stand. Out of the corner of her eye she saw her father studying his fingers and heard him announce, "All right. I guess you're not pregnant." What he had done made no sense, but he was freeing her. She ran to her room, slammed the door, dressed, and went to find Beedie.

Tina Korane resolved never to tell her mother of the incident. She assumed it had happened because her father was drunk or because for that single moment he had lost his senses. She could not believe it would happen again. She was only partially right. While Michael Korane never actually forced himself on his daughter again, he did not stop leering at her and occasionally following her with a look on his face that she had never seen. Beedie urged her to tell her mother but Tina was afraid of what might happen. Perhaps they would take her father to jail or to a mental hospital. Beedie promised she would protect her friend but argued that Mrs. Korane had to know. Tina protested that it would mean they would get a divorce. Her mother must not be told.

By the end of the school year, Tina Korane had begun to cut classes frequently. Even Beedie was surprised, although Beedie often cut school with her. Both girls were spending more time with boys and staying out late every night of the week. Nothing their parents said could get them to change their habits. They would hold to their promise of being home by dinner time for several days, but gradually the old pattern would return and they would be out until after midnight. The Helzers and Koranes made their daughters stay away from one another, each family believing that their daughter's friend was the bad influence. But there was no way the girls could be separated. Whenever Michael attempted to lay down the law, Tina stared at him as if to say, "Push me too hard and I'll tell everyone what you did." He never made severe demands on his daughter, which only infuriated Madelaine. She called him weak and told him she was sick of his moping about the world. Maybe it would be better if he *did* drink. Michael replied that he was a weakling.

Kit Helzer, on the other hand, had grown ferocious in the way he handled his daughter. He waited up for Beedie every night, and, the moment she entered the house, he lit into her, haranguing her, threatening to disown her. The more Beedie's lateness and general disobedience continued, the more furious he became until finally he took to whipping her. In the most extraordinary way, Michael Korane's terrifying moment with his daughter had seemed to initiate the unraveling of two families and nobody could help them establish the equanimity they once appeared to possess. No one in the girls' school could offer suggestions. The girls' work spoke for itself; they were doing as badly as anyone could. They turned in none of their work, made no effort to improve. Nobody knew what they were doing, where they were.

Life for both families became unbearable. Michael Korane grew more depressed, Kit Helzer more furious, their wives less able to manage the most fundamental responsibilities. By Christmas, the two girls had been brought in front of their local probation officers on four different occasions. The first two times involved their absences from school. On another occasion they were involved in a fight in the school yard. The fight was started by several other girls, one of them notorious for her gang-style behavior, but Tina and Beedie earned a ride to the police station. On the fourth occasion, the probation committee appointed by the court investigated the girls' alleged involvement with a group of young people who had been stealing from neighborhood stores. The descriptions of the girls given by local shop-keepers matched Tina Korane and Beedie Helzer closely enough to merit a special meeting with the probation officers. Neither of the fathers accompanied his wife to the meeting.

Tina and Beedie denied knowing anything about the shoplifting. They had never shoplifted, they said; they knew no one who did. "Then what *do* you do when you cut class and stay out until three and four o'clock in the morning?" they were asked by the probation officer.

"We go to people's homes or sit in hamburger places until they close. Things like that."

Hoping to help a situation he felt to be as confusing as it was dangerous, probation officer Gordon Whaley suggested that the girls see a social worker together. Perhaps they had things they wanted to talk about. "What do you think about the idea?" he asked them.

There was no answer.

"I can't force you," he persisted.

Still no answer.

He had begun to lose his patience. "Well, let's try it then?"

At last Beedie spoke. "Is it part of the probation deal?"

Gordon Whaley shrugged. "Yeah, I'll make it part of the probation deal."

Together the girls saw Mrs. Barbara Miller four times; then they began missing sessions with her, just as Gordon Whaley feared they might. He had no solution for the Helzers and Koranes. "What's going to happen," he told Madelaine and Michael on one of his home visits, "is very simple. I'm going to get a call some night, and I'm going to be calling you. The call is going to say, 'We got two girls named Helzer and Korane locked up in a cell and they're in one whole lot of trouble.' I don't understand these two, but I got exactly ten million just like them running around all over this city. You better get ready and make sure your telephone's working."

Michael Korane said nothing. His wife shook her head as if to say, "We've tried everything. Something snapped. Something went wrong."

Matthew Korane listened to Mr. Whaley for a while, then felt himself getting scared, and walked away. In the living room he tripped over a wire, pulling down a lamp. The noise startled everyone. Michael rushed into the room, saw the lamp, still burning, lying on the floor unbroken. He smacked Matthew hard on the buttocks. Matthew screamed. Madelaine entered the room, saw what had happened, and immediately grew angry with her husband. "For Chrissakes it was only an accident," she blurted out, trying somehow to comfort her son. Gordon Whaley glanced quickly at the family he knew to be living under extraordinary pressure and quietly excused himself. When the front door closed, Matthew ran to his room, Michael left the house by way of the kitchen door, and Madelaine Korane sat on the red Naugahyde chair near the window and wept. Periodically she raised her head and gazed at the telephone, half expecting the call Mr. Whaley had predicted to come that very instant.

The call did come in March, early in the morning. Madelaine Korane had been dreaming of a trip she had taken to a warm island. The family was vacationing together, although it appeared that she had more than her actual number of children. No matter, they were staying at a beautiful seaside hotel overlooking the most glorious clear blue water she had ever seen. In the dream, as she is walking along the water's edge, she tells her husband that this must be a dream. It's just too good to be true. But Michael, who looks more handsome than ever before in his life, tells her it is no dream, it is as real as the sand and the water and the wicked prices of the hotel they selected from the travel brochures. Madelaine looks at him, expecting him to be angry over the cost of the vacation. Instead, he is grinning broadly, his expression telling her not to worry about money but to enjoy their life together.

Far down the beach she sees another family coming toward them. She recognizes them to be the Helzers. They too look extremely happy. She can tell that Kit is entertaining them with one of his zany songs or stories. Made-laine is especially pleased to notice that when Tina and Beedie realize the other is on the island, they choose not to run ahead to embrace, but to stay with their own families until everyone comes together.

It was four thirty in the morning. The March night was freezing, the bedroom damp and chilly. Michael was aroused by the telephone but too sleepy to answer it. Madelaine had to step out of bed and go into the living room. On realizing that the beach scene had been a dream, she began weeping. She kept weeping throughout the conversation with an offi-cer named Archibald, who informed her that Tina and Beedie had been arrested late the previous afternoon. Mrs. Korane was advised to come to the station as soon as she could. Bail had not been set. "Did she have a husband?" the officer wondered.

"Of course," she answered.

"Well, bring him along too. You've got a real problem."

What followed that morning became more dreamlike to Madelaine Korane than her dream of the expensive seaside resort. Tina and Beedie had been arrested while drinking tea in a diner nine miles away in a part of the city known for its factories and light industries. There was no reason they would have chosen to enter this neighborhood except to be a part of the armed robbery of an all-night service station, which was what they had been arrested for. Accord-ing to the service station attendant, Neil Feld, the girls and three boys had driven into the station just after midnight on Friday night. They had requested gasoline. The girls, he said, were sitting in the front seat with one of the boys; the other two boys were in the back seat. When Mr. Feld stuck his head into the car window asking to be paid, the driver pro-duced a gun, ordered him to retreat into the office, and then hit him on the head. Before getting knocked unconscious, however, Mr. Feld heard the driver called by the name of

Manny or Money. He also got a good look at the two girls.

Upon regaining consciousness, the attendant discovered the station had been robbed of slightly more than one hundred dollars. He called the police and gave them a detailed description of his assailants. All of this took place at two o'clock in the morning. Later in the afternoon of that same day, Tina and Beedie were arrested. They were with one of the boys who Neil Feld claimed had been sitting in the back seat. Tina and Beedie told the police they had nothing to do with the robbery, that they were nowhere near the service station, and they had never heard of anyone named Manny or Money. But the attendant insisted they were the girls who had been in the car, and while he remembered only the boy Manny having a gun, nothing he saw would indicate that Tina or Beedie had been coerced to take part in the robbery. As best as he could remember, the girls had shown no surprise when Manny pulled out his gun. They had not called out to him to stop, as one of the boys had done.

Tina Korane and Beedie Helzer were arrested at four o'clock in the afternoon. The police notified Madelaine Korane twelve hours later—early Sunday morning. Tina's absence from the house went unnoticed, as presumably she was staying with Beedie for the weekend. Similarly, Beedie had told her parents that she would be staying with Tina. When Michael and Kit asked the police why it was that they had not been notified at once of their daughters' arrest, they were told that it had taken twelve hours to get the girls to reveal their parents' names and addresses. "Believe me," the arresting officer said, "I don't want no kids in my jail. Especially girls. We don't have proper facilities for girls."

"What the hell's the difference between a boys' jail and a girls' jail?" Kit Helzer quipped angrily.

"The question, *sir*," the officer admonished him, "is what

the hell are people like you doing half the time? I don't want anybody in these jails, especially no kids. You'll be begging to have them back here when you see where they go next."

It was just beginning to get light outside when Tina Korane was brought into the room where her parents waited. She embraced her mother and looked at her father with bewilderment and concern. She let him put his arm around her. Madelaine Korane noticed nothing of the tension between her daughter and her husband. She was unable to keep back her tears. Tina cried too, but Michael remained silent, the muscles of his face tight, as if he were preparing himself to say something or take some extreme action.

"I didn't do it," Tina kept sobbing. "I didn't do it. It wasn't like they said. I didn't do it, Mother. Neither did Beedie. It's all different. They're all lying."

Madelaine Korane comforted her daughter as she had when Tina was a little girl. She wished that she could push away the last years and have her only daughter be young again. Michael Korane remained standing, waiting for his daughter to tell her side of the story, waiting, too, to plan his own response. He was tired from being awakened so early, and hungry. He had an intense longing for pancakes and pork sausages, food he never ate in the morning. As a child he had watched his grandfather eat pork sausages for breakfast, seemingly by the dozen. Michael's mother would cook an entire package for her father, and Michael would sit alongside his grandfather and watch him push the sausages into his mouth, one after the other, without ever seeming to chew them, as if he were a machine. Michael loved the scene of his grandfather devouring sausages, but dreaded the notion that someday he might have to taste one of them; their odor was bad enough. Even his mother agreed. For his entire adult life, Michael's breakfast had been coffee and white toast and strawberry jam. When Madelaine ran out of strawberry jam, he ate no toast. Now he craved sausages. He was barely listening to his daughter's account.

According to Tina Korane, the episodes of the weekend could not have been more unlike what Neil Feld had reported. On Friday night, she and Beedie and a boy, Jack Binger, who was arrested with them, had been walking around downtown. By accident, they met a friend of Jack's, a young man named Tony Sizer, who was with his friend, the boy named Manny, whom Jack had not met before. While Manny and Tony Sizer did not seem particularly eager to be with Jack and his two girl friends, Manny's having a car appealed to Jack, who insisted they all go for a ride. Manny refused, saying it was a cold night and nobody in his right mind wanted to ride around doing nothing. Tina and Beedie did not care what the boys decided. All they knew was that it was cold and they were not dressed warmly enough.

After a long conversation, Manny agreed to take them in his car. The time was about nine thirty. After driving around downtown they went to a room which Tony shared with two other boys, both of whom were out for the evening. They began drinking; Tony had some dope for them to smoke. Then, as Tina recalled, they were back in the car, driving around in parts of the city she had never seen. At this point, Manny announced they needed gas, but since he had no intention of paying for it, they would have to rob a gasoline station. Jack and the two girls were terrified when Manny showed them his gun, but he laughed and assured them that while it was real, he never carried bullets for it. Still, they begged him to let them out of the car.

Suddenly Manny grew furious and told them to shut up. He warned Tina that if she opened her mouth he would shove the gun inside it and break every one of her teeth. He ordered Tony to watch Jack and to break his face if he even whispered. "You were the guys who wanted to drive around," he barked. "All this shit's your idea. I told you downtown I didn't want any part of you, especially no baby girls."

By this time Tina had begun to cry and Beedie was trembling. Jack Binger begged Manny to at least let the girls out of the car but Manny just grinned at him. "I'm a gentleman," he said unctuously. "I take my ladies home. I don't just drop them nowhere. I take 'em all home. You know what I mean? And I don't drop them 'til I'm finished with them." Even Tony had remarked that Manny was beginning to sound more like a character on a television show than a real person.

"This *is* a television show," Manny had shot back. "You never saw it? It's called rape the shit out of your friend's girl friends when they go 'round acting like they're big and important."

The robbery took place, Tina explained, exactly as the attendant had described it. The girls were too frightened to speak. Jack had been the one to call out and was promptly pounded in the stomach by Tony. They drove off and returned to Tony's apartment where Manny made them drink bourbon and beer until Beedie vomited. Tina herself was dizzy and nauseated. When everyone was drunk, Manny ordered Tony to undress the girls. He changed his mind about Beedie when he saw that she was practically unconscious, but as Tina was sitting with her eyes open, he concentrated on her. She tried to fight Tony off, but Manny walked behind her and held the butt of his gun in front of her face and warned her again how it would be no trouble for him to break her teeth. And if she didn't want him, he'd shove the gun up her cunt. His boots too if she didn't shut up.

Tina Korane stared at her father. He seemed to be sleeping, standing up with his eyes open, yet she knew he was listening to her.

Tony Sizer undressed her and then she was forced to lie

on the floor while Manny raped her. When he had finished he invited Tony to do it too while he held her, but Tony refused. "Just as well," Manny had said. "She wanted *me*, didn't you?" Tina knew he had no idea of her name. "You loved it. You wanted it all night, didn't you, girlie?" he taunted her, pulling his pants up while he stood over her. "And don't say you didn't 'cause it was *you* guys who started the invitation. What the hell are people walking around downtown for unless they're excited by trouble? Your friend Binger knows. That's why he pushed himself on me. 'Cause he wanted to impress you. Right? So, you impressed? Huh? Or just pregnant?" Manny had laughed and walked away.

Tina had fallen asleep. When she awoke she and Beedie were alone in the apartment. They heard people coming up the stairs and, fearing it was Manny returning, they went out the window and descended to the street on a fire escape. But they were too frightened to go home or telephone their parents. Beedie did not know what had happened to Tina. They walked around for several hours until they were so hungry they had to stop. Between them they had less than thirty cents. They decided to split up and go around asking people for a handout. Beedie returned in an hour with a dollar. The first person she asked gave her a quarter; the second had asked her good-naturedly, "Ain't it a little early in the morning for whores?" She immediately began to cry.

Early that afternoon they met Jack Binger, who offered to buy them tea at Toby's diner. They had barely sat down when four police officers placed them under arrest. Tony Sizer had been arrested that morning. Someone told the police how he had bragged about being with people who had robbed a service station. The boy named Manny had not been found. In fact, no one in the neighborhood seemed to know anybody named Manny, except for the Mexican youth, Emanuel Yepes, whom everyone called Manny. But clearly he was not the boy in question. There was absolutely no resemblance between the two boys.

Michael Korane could not explain the fury that overcame him when he heard Tina's story. It welled up in him four nights later as he was sitting in his kitchen wondering how he was going to get his daughter out of jail. He had been thinking of lawyers' fees, and the possibility that his daughter might remain behind bars for months before coming to trial. After all, she had had a poor record in school and with the probation office. Gordon Whaley had offered help, but everyone could see his pessimism. And Barbara Miller had left the city, her husband having taken a job in another state.

Michael left his home that March evening without speaking to anyone. But this was not unusual, for there was no one he spoke to. He had not been intimate with his wife for almost a year; their only conversations were about Tina. Indeed he had remarked once to Madelaine that if Tina hadn't gotten into trouble, they would have nothing to talk about. Madelaine was infuriated by this and called him an uncivilized animal. Yet there was a peculiar truth about his statement. They rarely spoke but instead put on what Madelaine called royal performances for the social workers and probation officers. Tina might have been finding ways to aggravate them only to keep them together, united in a concern over her. So there was no one to speak to when Michael bundled himself up and left the house that night with no particular purpose in mind.

It was eleven thirty when he reached the pool hall on Western Avenue where a man at Regis Place said many of the local kids hung out. Michael had already visited half a dozen places where it was said the tougher boys went in the evening. At Minny's Pool Hall he asked again the question he had asked all evening, and his manner remained cordial:

"Could you please tell me, is there a boy that comes here that anyone might know named Manny something? No problems, just wanted to say a few words to him. He's friends with my daughter."

The young man at Minny's had the first encouraging response of the night. "I got a Manny," he said. "Kid over there with a green sweater. He's here more than he's anywhere. Kid practically lives here."

"Would you know, by any chance," Michael Korane asked slowly, his body calm in a way that he had never known, "whether this Manny drives a car?"

"Drive a car? The kid does two things, man. Shoots pool and tinkers with his car. You looking for a mechanic?"

Michael Korane laughed modestly. "Might just be at that," he said. "Thanks for your time," he concluded with exaggerated politeness.

Little Manny Yepes, Emanuel Francisco Yepes, born in southwest Texas, moved to Oklahoma, New Mexico, Ohio, and Indiana by the time he was nine, then to the east coast, then back to the southwest, then back to the east coast again. A cheerful boy, not a jokester or troublemaker, just a pleasant sort of young man. You had to like Manny Yepes. Just looking at him made you feel good. That's what they said. Everybody knew him. They knew him by his face, by his slight frame, by the Kelly-green sweater he wore three hundred and sixty-five days a year about which, when they razzed him about it, he would say, "I'm breaking it in, I'm breaking it in." That would silence everyone. That and the lovely smile, the beautiful white teeth, the warm brown skin, the shiny black hair that seemed to comb itself.

Everyone knew little Manny Yepes, and he loved being known, being a celebrity even. So he wasn't surprised when the sad-looking man in his mid-forties came asking for him at Minny's that night and inquired if he were *the* Manny and then wondered if they might speak for a moment outside. Everybody did this with Manny Yepes. Everybody had a deal, a proposition, because Manny Yepes was for real, he knew people, he'd never steer anyone wrong. Someone was always asking Manny Yepes to go outside for a little talk in private, even the police, because in that neighborhood when some young person was accused of a crime and the police wanted to know if the kid was telling the truth and the kid had mentioned Manny Yepes, the police knew they would get the truth. Manny Yepes was genuine, honest. If the man who wanted to talk with him now was a cop, the man would get the truth. For Manny Yepes had one motto: If you don't want me to go to the cops, don't tell me about your trouble. And the kids respected him for it. So he went outside with the man he suspected of being a policeman and he answered yes to the question, "Do you have a car?" and he answered yes when asked if he knew Tina Korane. Then there was a long pause, neither man speaking, their eyes searching one another out like boxers before a fight. Then little Manny Yepes was lying face down in the snow, unconscious from a blow to his head with a two by four, the blood splattering his Kelly-green sweater. Michael Korane walked away, his revenge taken out on an innocent boy.

Several men found Manny Yepes and within minutes he was on his way to the hospital. Two of his friends went with him. They wanted to telephone his parents but suddenly realized they had no idea where Manny lived. The boys waited in the hospital all night and the following morning to learn the extent of his injury. As it turned out, his hearing was impaired but his left eye regained normal vision. A nineteen-stitch cut on the side of his head also healed properly, although when his hair falls a certain way the scar is visible.

Manny Yepes says he is lucky. He never saw the blow; he never felt pain—only wetness and warmth. He remembers going outside with the man, but not the man's face. Other boys in the pool hall remembered Michael Korane well. They could easily have given the police a description of him had not Michael turned himself in. Thirty minutes after the attack on Manny Yepes, he admitted everything, and, surprisingly, confessed that he knew from the moment he first saw Manny that this could not possibly have been the boy he had been hunting. But he could not control himself. As he broke down weeping, he asked a policeman whether they ever put fathers in the same jails with their daughters.

One year later, Michael Korane sat in jail, convicted on a charge of manslaughter. His admission that he knew the Yepes boy was not the person he sought brought him a lighter sentence than he might have received. At his sentencing, the judge made certain to say that Mr. Korane was in desperate need of psychiatric care. He assumed that Michael would be treated while in jail. Progress along these lines would surely lessen the sentence. In truth, Michael was pleased that he would be seeing someone. For a long time, he had wanted to speak with a psychiatrist but didn't know how to go about it, or even admit that he wanted to. After one year in prison, Michael Korane had been seen by a staff psychiatrist exactly once. He was assigned to a group psychotherapy program, which he attended for one evening. When he saw all the other men who would be listening to him, he refused to continue. He was promised individual treatment as soon as a doctor was available.

Still, as Kit Helzer said on learning what Michael Korane did, "When you want to believe something, you don't listen to the truth, you don't give a hoot or damn about the truth. Old Michael wanted revenge, he wanted to get even for what happened to his daughter, even though to hear Madelaine tell the story, he didn't even look like he was listening to Tina when she told them about it. Those goddam punk sons of bitches, I wish to Christ Korane would have told me what he was going to do. I'd have gone with him and busted up a few faces myself, even though Beedie, thank the good Lord, wasn't in trouble. You don't blame a guy for doing that, mistake or no mistake. You don't blame a father. The father of that kid Yepes, he ain't got all that much of a gripe coming. He can understand it. Deep down in him, he can understand. He knows what it's like to be a father and learn your kid has been raped by some goddam maniac, some perverted animal who the police and the whole goddam society lets run around because they can't make these charges stick, or the evidence is what they call circumstantial. I don't believe in taking law into your own hands. But the man is her *father*. My kid told me this guy named Manny raped her, I'd have found the first punk kid on the street whose name even sounded like that, Danny, Canny, Fanny, I'd have killed him for Chrissakes. What Korane did shows one thing: He loves his daughter."

Tina Korane and Beedie Helzer were sentenced for their participation in the armed robbery of the filling station and for seven convictions of shoplifting. The judge told them he hoped a year in prison would calm them down and put them on the right track. He said they had been leading their lives as though they could sweet-talk their way out of any difficulty. Being in jail was intended as a deterrent. If their behavior was good they would be released in six months. There was only one problem. They had waited for trial for almost seventeen months. Furthermore, Beedie Helzer had been sentenced to prison in a different state on the grounds that there was no room in the prison to which Tina was assigned. Tina reported, however, that there were "millions of empty cells" in her prison. Presumably, Beedie was shipped away in order to separate the two girls.

"I didn't think I'd ever get over them moving Beedie out," Tina Korane said during her stay in prison. "Fact is, all of this has been like a dream. First that night with Manny, then the police, then waiting for the trial—I was so scared then I vomited every day, even when I didn't eat anything. Then coming out here. It's unbelievable. Nobody told me about what my father did 'til a lot later. Do you believe that? He'd gone to trial by the time I found out. I saw my mother almost every other day and she never told me. And they wouldn't let me see my brother or sister. Then finally my mother told me. I couldn't believe it. Such a stupid thing to do, pick on some innocent guy. I didn't even know him. I don't know why he told my father he knew me. I didn't even hear of him 'til they mentioned his name. But my father was crazy. He wanted to do something to make it better. Maybe he knew that he was the cause of it. But that isn't true either. I don't know what it is. Nobody can figure it out anymore. That's the only thing I'm sure of. Nobody can figure it out.

"Then my mother and my two aunts who come out here to visit me once in a while, you know, they all tell me, 'Tina, you'll see, it's all going to take care of itself. Everything'll get better,' My Aunt Helen, who's this busybody, always interested in other people's business—she loves it when people get in trouble 'cause it makes her life look better. *Her* children are the biggest misfits I've ever seen; they're worse than anybody I've ever met in here, I'll tell you *that* for sure. Anyway, she says to me, 'Tina, dear, it's like a big operation. But the scar's going to disappear. You'll see. Each day it gets littler and littler.' She doesn't know. Nobody knows. Nobody knows why anything happens. They got this psychologist in here who comes to see a bunch of us, maybe we've seen him ten times now, he's always asking, 'But what do *you* think started all the trouble? What do *you* think?' Well, how the hell should *we* know? If we knew we wouldn't be here, right? He ought to get together with my Aunt Helen. The two of them would make a perfect pair. He'd ask her,

'What do *you* think started all the trouble?' and she'd have a million answers for him. She knows everything. At least she thinks she does.

"Here's another wonderful thing about Helen. She comes out here—like it's maybe twenty miles from her home, right, and it takes her an hour one way to make the trip, right— but she'll sit and talk to my mother about her own life. They've just traveled together for over an hour, but when they see me they got to keep talking to themselves. Sometimes it's like they forget I'm even here. I figured out that maybe they're like that because they'd like to forget I'm here. It embarrasses them. Which I like a lot. Embarrasses *them?* They ought to ask *me* some time what it's like being in here—how it embarrasses *me*. Nobody knows that who hasn't been in prison. People on the outside, they think all of us are animals, that's why we're here, or we've lost our feelings. They say if we had feelings we wouldn't have done what we did to get in here in the first place. I suppose I can't blame nobody for thinking like that. How could they know unless they've been here? Just talking to prisoners isn't enough to find out. But still they think we don't like it, which is true, but that we get used to it. I mean, we aren't supposed to be embarrassed to see one another every day since all of us are in the same boat, you might say. People on the outside think we lose being embarrassed until we come on the outside, when we feel it all over again. We're supposed to be like the ex-con in the world with everybody else. They tell this story all the time about the two women who meet at this big, important party, you know, and each of them are married to big important men, and they were once together in the same cell. You believe it? Someone said it was a true story.

"Anyway, what I wanted to say was that we're embarrassed plenty being in here. Plenty. I know I am. All the time when I'm with people, even when I'm alone. Some nights, you know, I'll be lying in the bed, I don't hear nobody in the corridor or next to me. Everybody's sleeping. And I'll think to myself, I'd hate to have someone see me now, come looking in here, you know, 'cause they'd see right away I was in jail. It's really stupid. 'Course I'm in jail. Where else am I? Everybody sees where I am. But I guess maybe somewhere inside me I'm trying to pretend I'm not here, that none of it happened, that nobody will find out about me, or see me. Then sometimes I think, maybe I don't want 'em to see 'cause there's nothing I can do but look at 'em. I'm helpless. All I can do's stare at 'em, you know, and say, 'Okay, what the hell you want of me? You caught me. I'm in jail. I'm a jailbird. Right? Isn't that what you wanted me to say? Okay, so I admitted it. There's nothing in the world I can do about it neither, so leave me alone.'

"But I really am embarrassed. I don't want people to see me, like, how I am. Like, if you ask about me at my old school, they'll tell you, 'Tina Korane, she was a dummy. Didn't have a brain worth using. Doesn't surprise me at all she's in jail. Might just as well be there as anywhere else. She's a nothing.' I know they feel like that. I didn't give them any reason not to think that way. I'd be plenty embarrassed to go back to that school. I'd never go there. But I'm not as dumb as they think I am. I know I didn't work at school and Beedie and me were always in trouble, but I wasn't dumb. Some of the kids were—some of them, I mean, they were *really* dumb. But I wasn't dumb like them. I was smart. I don't know about how I am now, but I was smart then, plenty. They just didn't know, and I never could figure out a way to show them, but I was smart. This place is just like school, making everybody feel ashamed of what they've done and who they are. At school I used to walk around thinking people were thinking, well, there goes the dummy. Wonder where she's going now. In here I think they're thinking, well, there goes little Miss Jail Bird. If she weren't in here with the walls she'd be out there in the big, wide world getting into trouble. Sometimes I wish I could be somebody else. I never felt that before coming here. Even with all that happened to me, and there was a lot, I never wanted to be anybody but me. Least I never thought about being anybody else. But in here, boy, I think about it all the time. I wish I were the guard, I wish I were the director, I wish I were the mailman, I wish I were the doctor . . . the doctor. Got to tell you about the doctor.

"I had this pain one morning. It was really bad. I thought I was going to have to have my appendix out. So I told the guard instead of going to breakfast. Well, that morning they had a doctor right there. I mean I was in his office like five minutes after I told the guard. Lots of the women, you know, they fake being sick so they can get attention. I did that once too, only that was after this time when I was really sick. Anyway, I'm in his office and he was very nice. He wasn't being fresh or anything. He asked me a whole lot of questions, like if I'd been in a hospital before and did I have operations and what was my worst sickness. Then he told me I had to take my clothes off. I was nervous about that. I mean, I knew sooner or later he had to look at me, 'specially since my pain was down there, you know. But I did it. I acted like the world's biggest fool folding my clothes so neatly, as if they were such special clothes or something instead of the junk they make us wear which they iron and wash so much it's like the clothes are made of iron. Then the doctor told me to lie down on this tiny little table and I started to cry and cry, and my body was shaking. It was terrible. I couldn't think what it was. I never was like that before. First I thought, maybe it's because this is the first time I'd been like that, naked, you know, in front of a man since that time with that guy Manny. Maybe it was all coming back. So I thought real hard about that, 'cause I didn't want the doctor to think I was crazy, and I figured if that was why I was shaking, I'd stop, I'd be all right. But I kept on shaking

"So then I thought, maybe I'm going crazy like this because of the time with my father, which I always thought was the beginning of all my trouble. You know, doctors, my father, sticking their fingers in me, telling me what's supposed to be wrong with me. That time with my father, I never talked about it to nobody, but it was really spooky, the spookiest. I didn't know what to make of what he was doing. I'd heard of fathers making it with their daughters. I even knew a girl once who loved doing it with her father. She said she couldn't wait 'til he'd get home and get rid of her old lady, send her off to the store somewhere. Another girl in here had a cell near me for about a month. I told her about my old man 'cause she asked me what my parents were doing, how they were taking my being in here, you know. She said she'd made it with her father and one of her uncles. Fact, she once took a room in a motel with her father. You believe that? They checked in like they were man and wife, or like she was his mistress. She said the two of 'em would get drunk out of their minds and go at it pretending they weren't who they were. She'd pretend she was with some famous movie star and her father would get off because he was with a young chick. Believe *that?*

"Well, it wasn't like that with *my* father. When he did that number about me being pregnant, I didn't imagine he was no movie star. I was conscious all the time. I kept thinking, it ain't happening. Somebody come in here and tell me this isn't happening. Daddy, come in from the other room and tell me this man here isn't my real father. So when I started shaking with the doctor I decided maybe that's what it was, my father scene all over again, although I never made it with my father. He didn't go that far, 'though I sure thought he was. After that one thing, you could have believed anything would happen. Can you imagine the five of us sitting at that table in the kitchen with people asking to pass the salt and the mashed potatoes so politely, and the day before he had done what he done? I knew my parents weren't having sex. I knew my mother'd closed him out. She never told me. Neither did he, of course, but I heard them all the time—paper walls home we lived in. I knew what they were trying to keep from us. You have all that stuff on your mind, you don't go to school ready to concentrate on anything.

"You know why I was shaking with that doctor? I figured it out. It didn't help me that much, but it calmed me down. You ready for this? I didn't want him to see me as a prisoner. How's that for being crazy? That's what it was too. I know it doesn't make any sense, but that's what I thought. With my clothes on I could pretend just to be a patient, or some other person. But when I had to take my clothes off I couldn't hide anything from him, and I mean *anything*, so it made the embarrassment all over again for being what I was, and when you're in jail, all you are is someone in jail. No more being a student or someone's daughter or someone's sister. All you are is a prisoner, and that always embarrasses me a whole lot.

"Did you notice I just said, 'I *was* in jail'? As if I weren't in jail anymore. I wonder if I'll ever feel I'm not in jail, even when I'm out of here. I wonder if when I'm a hundred years old—if I get that far—and I haven't been in jail for eighty years, if I'll really feel I'm not in jail. I wonder if anyone who's been in here ever feels free again. I doubt it. I'll know soon enough, but I doubt it.

"I know they have to put you in jail when you break the law, though with me I got stuck for a lot of things that weren't my doing. Like, I'm in jail and my father's in jail, which is great for the rest of the family, right? But they never heard of that guy Manny, the real Manny. And you can bet the second I get out of here I'll run into him. He'll come looking for me to say he's sorry or something, and disappear. Guys like that, what he did, I'll bet he doesn't even think he should go to jail, especially for what he did to me. Those guys don't think that's a crime. They just see it as some form of perverted sex, but it's no crime to them. Still, even with guys like that, I don't think jail would do them any good. It can only hurt you. It can't do anything, not for me, not for my father, not even for Manny the Monster. Maybe with someone my father's age it isn't all that bad since his life is pretty much over anyway, but with young kids, it's pretty serious. But then, so is sticking up a gasoline station. But then *I* didn't do that, did I? I mean, I don't approve of shoplifting or cutting school. You have to be punished 'cause they can't let people get away with it, but jail? I don't think so. Not jail. These places are for the maddest killers in the world. They aren't for punk kids like me. I mean, I'm just a girl and they got me in here treating me like I was a world-famous criminal. That's got to be a little lopsided, don't it? I don't deserve all this. Nobody deserves what you get in here. Nothing's worth all this. Nothing in the world from the time it started to the time it's going to end.

"Talking about it is getting to be so hard for me. It's not getting any easier. I thought it would be after all these months, but it isn't. I can't believe what it's like for my father or my mother or anyone in the family. It must be harder on them too. Every day that nothing changes, like it never does in here, it gets harder. I got to find a way to get my mind off it, you know what I mean. Like getting myself to relax. But getting my mind off it means getting myself to stop thinking about my *life*, and what else do I have to think about but my life? God, I see everything getting thinner and thinner, blacker and blacker. Like I was losing a lot of weight all at once and there was less and less light in the world. It's getting thinner and thinner every day in here, and blacker and blacker. It will never be the way it was. I can't make things good again, no matter what I try. Even if I tried, really tried I mean, I don't know that anybody or anything in the outside would let things get better for me. I suppose the best thing for me to do is pretend that when I get out of here, my life will be over; then everything that happens from then on will happen either in heaven or hell. If it's good it will be like heaven; if it's bad, it will be like hell. Except when you've been in jail, there's only one way it can be. So there's no way out for me, is there? I've really sort of had it, haven't I? I can't even vote yet or get a drink in a bar and I've had it. Forever, whatever that's supposed to mean. They take *that* away from you too, in here. There's no forever in here, no long ago either. Just rotten old right now, and a lot of rotten old right nows to come. Is this really me? Really?"

Epilogue: What Can Be Done?

Several years have passed since I first began speaking with children in jail, some of whom appear in this book. They have not been happy years for the children, even though many of them have been released and now are once again living in their old communities. Some returned to school, some found jobs; others have been employed for brief periods but find that the experience of jail has not only hurt them psychologically but jeopardized their already meager opportunities. In addition to the deaths reported in this volume, several other children with whom I met regularly have died since their release from jail. Two were suicides, three the victims of physical illness. Physicians assured me, however, that the illnesses were exacerbated by the time spent in jail, for not only was the experience of incarceration debilitating, it was obvious that the children were not receiving proper medical attention. Their medical records, retained by the prisons, were wholly inadequate, almost suspect, given the paucity of information in them.

With the help of lawyers, physicians, social workers, and other community workers, we were able to get a good number of children out of jail and into so-called rehabilitation programs, like halfway houses. Almost all the children illegally held in adult jails and in detention centers awaiting trial were released. In some cases, we were able to reopen the trials of certain children who, we were convinced, were innocent. In one instance, this work resulted in a mistrial and the child was freed. In a second instance, it was shown that a boy, whose case is not reported in this book, had been a victim of mistaken identity. He had spent fourteen months in jail. In a third, a boy was again sent before a juvenile court judge willing to hear his case. He had admitted committing a minor offense but had become a model prisoner. The judge released him to the care of his aunt, because his own home was found to be "too unstable and inappropriate." For several weeks he complained of feeling lost and disoriented. He hated jail, but felt he had no real home outside. Within two months of his release he committed suicide.

Unfortunately, the accounts of children in jail—only a few of which I have reported here—rarely have happy endings. To be sure, there are stories of children who transcend their experience in jail and become, as we say, law-abiding and contributing citizens. But the majority of the cases with which I have been involved almost invariably reveal children who have been deeply hurt by serving a jail term. As I said in the introduction, movements for prison reform hardly imply condoning the criminal acts of the child. But my own impression is that the jail experience may well be called traumatic. Granted, trauma normally implies a sudden shock for which the person is wholly unprepared and jail isn't necessarily experienced in this fashion, although often it is. How many times I have heard: I was never prepared for this—I never believed jail could be this way. The concept of trauma seems appropriate to these cases because the delicate tissues of psychological and physical protection are shattered, if not wholly destroyed, by being in jail, and recovery, typically, is slow, very slow. Years after a person's release, the psychological and physical symptoms resulting from incarceration may still be detected. Phobias and nightmares are commonly reported by ex-prisoners. One observes facial tics, extreme nail biting, stammering, learning difficulties, bowel and bladder problems, sexual inadequacy, and a host of physical symptoms in young people who by all reports entered jail medically normal.

Naturally, it will be argued by some that many children who wind up in jail are either biologically or psychologically disturbed, to some degree, before entering. It is this disturbance, the argument continues, that relates to their original involvement with criminal activities. It is my own impression, and I am no expert on this subject, that research will eventually confirm the notion that biological or psychological predispositions for criminality mean little in the absence of an environmental or sociological context. Family life, social life, community attachments, interpersonal bonds, cultures, milieus, "the scene," whatever one chooses to call it, inevitably plays a crucial role in the development of a child, both physically and psychologically, and thus a prominent role in the child's behavior and sense of morality. Indeed, the enormous literature on juvenile delinquency points again and again to the overpowering significance of the social world in the life of the child involved with crime. It is no accident that the preponderance of so-called delinquents comes from the lower reaches of society, where life is far more difficult and where authority and institutions are far less lenient, tolerant, and supportive.

We cannot remind ourselves often enough that the experience of jail enhances the likelihood of the child committing further crimes. Jail is rarely rehabilitative and typically destructive. Thus, it is not inappropriate to begin jail reform programs with the notion of abolishing jails, as they are presently defined, for children. The problem of reform, as we well know, is a complex one. Almost any position that one takes can be thoughtfully argued or supported with the results of already completed studies and investigations. Furthermore, some would agree that the solution to children in jail already exists in the structure and philosophy of the juvenile court system, despite the fact that in many instances this system fails to work efficiently, or even humanely. Still, the mechanism is there. As the authors of *Children in Adult Jails* * write, juvenile courts "can play a significant role by refusing to order jail detention in violation of state laws and constitutional rights of children. Their insistence on protecting such rights would do much to force the legislative and executive branches of state governments to provide alternatives to jail incarceration of children."

Let me carry on with the recommendations of the Children's Defense Fund report. Juvenile courts, the authors state, must make legal procedures absolutely clear to all law enforcement officers. They should require that all children arrested be properly screened and that detention hearings be held within twenty-four hours from the time of the arrest. Juvenile courts should closely review all complaints and oversee not only the cases with which they are involved but the facilities that eventually house the child. They should be, among other things, agencies involved in the collection

---

* Published in 1976 by the Children's Defense Fund of the Washington Research Project, 1763 R Street, NW, Washington, D.C. 20009.

of information about the children brought to their attention, but, importantly, they must make this information available to those who would act on behalf of the child.

So some of the burden rests on the already elaborate and complex machinery of the juvenile court system. Some of the burden rests as well on state and federal governments. Where there is a concentration of power, there is machinery for change and amelioration, just as there is machinery for destruction and oppression. The federal government can pass legislation that would prevent the incarceration of people under the age of eighteen. Indeed, the government would do well to enforce laws already on the books, which greatly curtail the degree of incarceration. It is clear that the arrangement presently established between federal or state governments and the jails will only encourage the incarceration of children.

In addition, appropriate state and federal agencies must continually collect information about juvenile incarceration and monitor jails as well as programs offered as alternatives to jail. Site visits must be made regularly and often; reports must be written; one must listen to the jailers and the jailed and take seriously their accounts of the experience of children in jail. As the Children's Defense Fund report indicates, it is necessary that we know about the behavior of the police, the courts, and those in charge of jails. We must know as well the wording of the law in various states and the quality of facilities in various jails. We must know just who is being jailed, and their physical and psychological status. And we must inform state and federal agencies, like the Law Enforcement Assistance Administration, the Department of Justice, or the National Council on Crime and Delinquency, of all instances where the child's rights have not been assiduously preserved and honored. The data collected, in turn, must be made available to child advocates and lawyers, or anyone who would work on behalf of and for the protection of the children.

Again and again we hear of proposals that appear to contain idealistic if not utopian wording. There is always need for such wholly revolutionary schemes, for without them we remain without vision and without dreams. I am not a particularly good dreamer. I do my best to attend to what people are saying, but when it comes to policymaking, I find my proposals limited and unimaginative. Partly this is because my talents, alas, are limited. Partly too, it is because I cannot seem to get beyond the realities of existing structures, like prisons, as well as the present state of legislation and law enforcement. I heartily advocate the notion that children must not be placed in jail, so let us tear down jails to be certain that not one more child will be incarcerated. But even as I write these words, I realize that alternatives to jail may well become tomorrow's jails. I know too that reform movements of this type are difficult to begin, and slow, dreadfully slow in making a difference.

Inevitably, as the Children's Defense Fund report makes plain, interim measures must be outlined. For example, as we work to close down jails, we must investigate and correct for the disproportionate number of minority children in jail. We must also insist on adequate facilities and the proper treatment of children during their term in jail. Naturally, it may be asked, can we even speak of "proper treatment" in the context of children in jail? I think we can. In my conversations I have heard from many young people an admission that they deserve to be punished for what they have done. They deserve, and possibly want, treatment, rehabilitation, a different type of education, a chance to be helped. They despise jail, but they also fear that the return to their homes and neighborhoods might encourage them to pursue their old ways, which they now would like to abandon. The experience and stigma of jail will never help them, but there are forms of institutional living that might, and the children themselves are willing to try. They have their own dreams and wishes, but their childhood has taught them that one pays a big price for freedom. I believe that, in the main, they want nothing for nothing.

As I have said, a matter of limited talents keeps me from being a major contributor to policy formation. There is probably a temperamental constraint as well: I dread the idea of designing life-styles or programs for other people. At times, I content myself with the notion that some people write policy so that they don't have to meet the very people whose lives they are hoping to reform. Presently, it is my impression that there are more policymakers than people willing to befriend children in jail or children about to enter or leave jail. For me, the act of befriending, and inevitably working on the *child's* behalf, is the noble enterprise. Without law and social structure to support the child advocate, the work is impossible. But even existing laws and legislation are sufficient to enhance the work and position of the advocate. The support systems, as they say, have already been constructed; it's the children who now must receive our attention. And they are special children, for it goes without saying that their backgrounds have been difficult and some of their behavior a challenge to an ideology and a definition of morality that many of the rest of us uphold.

Like all child advocacy work, befriending and supporting a jailed child rattles our protective devices and shakes our vulnerabilities. It is not safe work or calm work, and, in our culture, it is not held too valuable, at least according to the normal social criteria of value. It brings little prestige, little money, no power. I don't even know that I would call it rewarding work, since one never feels work of this sort has been satisfactorily completed. Always there is more to do, another child to see, another case to work on. But if one asks, demands even, that a government undertake certain action, then one in effect is asking only that people take action, which means, or should mean, that one should undertake the action oneself. I can make visits to jails. I can work for their abolition. I can assess an institution's facilities. I can listen to the accounts of jailed children, as well as their custodians. I can befriend another human being. So, in a most selfish way, to advocate children's rights is to safeguard my own.

Children's Rights Organizations

For those who want to explore the possibility of becoming a child advocate

Advance Foundation, Inc.
3502 S. Normandie Avenue
Los Angeles, Calif. 90007

American Civil Liberties Union
85 Fifth Avenue
New York, N.Y. 10011

American Friends Service Committee
112 S.. 16th Street
Philadelphia, Pa. 19102

Association of Volunteer Bureaus of America
P.O. Box 7253
Kansas City, Mo. 64113

Center for Law and Social Policy
1600 20th Street, N.W.
Washington, D.C. 20009

Center for the Study of Student Citizenship, Rights, and Responsibility
1145 Germantown Street
Dayton, O. 45408

Center on Human Policy
216 Ostrom Avenue
Syracuse, N.Y. 13210

Child Welfare League of America
44 East 23rd Street
New York, N.Y. 10010

Children's Defense Fund
1763 R Street, N.W.
Washington, D.C. 20009

Children's Foundation
1026 17th Street, N.W.
Washington, D.C. 20036

Citizen's Committee for Children
112 East 19th Street
New York, N.Y. 10003

Coordinating Council for Handicapped Children
407 S. Dearborn Street
Chicago, Ill. 60605

The Council for Exceptional Children State-Federal Clearinghouse
1920 Association Drive
Reston, Va. 22091

Day Care and Child Development Council of America
1426 H Street, N.W.
Suite 340
Washington, D.C. 20005

Education Exploration Center
3104 16th Avenue S.
Minneapolis, Minn. 55407

Freedom Through Equality, Inc.
152 West Wisconsin Avenue
Milwaukee, Wis. 53203

Health-Policy Advisory Committee (PAC)
17 Murray Street
New York, N.Y. 10007

International Association of Parents of the Deaf
(IAPD)
Silver Spring, Md.

Robert F. Kennedy Fellows Program for the Rights of Children
1054 31st Street, N.W.
Washington, D.C. 20007

LEAP (A community action project)
540 East 13th Street
New York, N.Y.

Massachusetts Advocacy
2 Park Square
Boston, Mass. 02116

Mental Health Law Project
84 Fifth Avenue
New York, N.Y. 10011
1751 N Street, N.W.
Washington, D.C. 20036

Mental Patients Liberation Project
P.O. Box 89
West Sommerville, Mass. 02114

National Center for Child Advocacy Department of HEW, Office of the Secretary
P.O. Box 1182
Washington, D.C. 20013
A list of advocacy centers throughout the country may be obtained through this address.

National Center for Law and the Handicapped
1235 N. Eddy Street
South Bend, Ind. 46617

National Center for Volunteer Action
1735 I Street, N.W.
Washington, D.C. 20006

National Clearinghouse for Legal Services
Northwestern University Law School
710 N. Lake Shore Drive
Chicago, Ill. 60611

National Committee for Children and Youth
1145 19th Street, N.W.
Washington, D.C. 20036

National Council on the Rights of the Mentally Impaired
1600 20th Street, N.W.
Washington, D.C. 20009

National Juvenile Law Center
St. Louis University School of Law
3642 Lindell Boulevard
St. Louis, Mo. 63108

National Legal Aide and Defender Association
National Law Office
1601 Connecticut Avenue, N.W.
Washington, D.C. 20009

National Welfare Rights Organization
1419 H Street, N.W.
Washington, D.C. 20005

New Nation Seed Fund
P.O. Box 4026
Philadelphia, Pa. 19118
Funding agency for new schools, concerned primarily with low-income students.

The Office of Mental Retardation Coordination
Department of HEW
Washington, D.C. 20201

Organizer's Book Center
P.O. Box 21066
Washington, D.C. 20009

The President's Committee on Mental Retardation
Seventh and D Streets, S.W.
Washington, D.C. 20201

Social Advocates for Youth
315 Montgomery Street
Suite 1014
San Francisco, Calif. 94104

Summerhill Collective
137A West 14th Street
New York, N.Y. 10011

Work Force
Vocations for Social Change
P.O. Box 13
Canyon, Calif. 94516
4911 Telegraph Avenue
Box C
Oakland, Calif. 94609

Youth Organizations United
912 6th Street, N.W.
Washington, D.C. 20001

EASTERN